PILLARS OF MAGYAR POETRY

Hungarian poems selected and translated by Paul Sohar

Červená Barva Press
Somerville, Massachusetts

Červená Barva Press
P.O. Box 440357
W. Somerville, MA 02144

www.cervenabarvapress.com

Bookstore: www.thelostbookshelf.com

Production: Allison O'Keefe

Cover art: Jan ten Broeke (1930-2019)

ISBN: 978-1-950063 86-4

Library of Congress Control Number: 2023944760

CONTENTS

Foreword 3

WARS OF OLD (1550-1890)

Bálint Balassi

SOLDIER SONG IN PRAISE OF THE FRONTLINES (*Egy katonaének; in laudem confiniorum*) 13

Mihály Csokonai

TO HOPE (*Reményhez*) 14
HESITANT REQUEST (*Tartozkodó kérelem*) 16
LETHE 16

Sándor Petőfi

NATIONAL CALL (*Nemzeti dal*) 17
MY WINTER IN DEBRECZEN (*Egy telem Debreczenben*) 19
SEPTEMBER (*Szeptember*) 20
LIBERTY AND LOVE (*Szabadság, szerelem...*) 20

János Arany

THE WORLD (*A világ*) 21
THE ANCIENT TOWER (*Az ó torony*) 22
SHIPWRECKED (*A hajótörött*) 24
AT HOME (*Itthon*) 26
MY HOPE (*Reményem*) 27
TRIAL BY THE CORPSE (*Tetemre hivás*) 29
CIVILIZATION (*Civilizáció*) 32

WARS OF DECLINE (1905-1923)

Endre Ady

ON NEW WATERS I SAIL (*Új vizeken járok*) 35
THE LADY OF THE CASTLE IN WHITE (*A vár fehér asszonya*) 36
WHEN THE PYRE DIES (*Hunyhat a máglya*) 37
MATING ON THE AUTUMN LEAVES (*Héja-nász az avaron*) 38
LEDA'S HEART (*A Léda szíve*) 39
ON THE SHORES OF THE BLUE SEA (*A kék tenger partján*) 40
THE BLACK-LACQUERED CONCERT GRAND (*A fekete zongora*) 40
TO WEEP AND WEEP (*Sírni, sírni, sírni*) 41
THE COUSIN OF DEATH (*A Halál rokona*) 42
MY BRIDE (*Az én menyasszonyom*) 43
THE SONG OF A CHEERFUL FUNERAL (*Vidám temetés éneke*) 45
LONGING TO BELONG (*Szeretném ha szeretnének*) 46
IN THE WASTELAND OF HUNGARY (*A magyar ugaron*) 47
DUEL WITH THE HOG-HEADED MISTER BIG (*Harc a Nagyúrral*) 48
REMEMBERING A SUMMER NIGHT (*Emlékezés egy nyár-éjszakára*) 50
CADAVER ON THE WHEATFIELD (*Hulla a búzaföldön*) 51
THE JÁNOS OF FAIRY TALES (*A mesebeli János*) 52
MY DOUBTING MAGYAR SOUL (*Kétkedő, magyar lelkem*) 54
THE MUSIC OF AUTUMN (*Az ősz muzsikája*) 55
THE NEW HARVEST SONG (*Új arató ének*) 56
LEADING THE DEAD BRIGADE (*A halottak élén*) 57
CHRONICLE SONG FROM 1918 (*Krónikás ének 1918-ból*) 59
CHRISTMAS (*Karácsony*) 60
GIVING THANKS (*Hála adás*) 62
THE MAGYAR MESSIAHS (*A magyar messiások*) 63
THE LAST SHIPS (*Az utolsó hajók*) 64

Dezső Kosztolányi

HUNGARIAN POETS CRY OUT TO THE POETS OF EUROPE IN 1919
(*Magyar költők sikolya Európa költőihez 1919-ben*) 65
THE BEGGAR OF TEARS (*Könnyek koldusa*) 66
A FLAG (*Zászló*) 67

Mihály Babits

THE YOUNG SOLDIER (*Fiatal katona*) 68
EVENING QUESTIONS (*Esti kérdés*) 69
HEGESO'S STELE (*Hegeso sírja*) 71
DEPARTURE FOR OLD AGE (*Indulás az öreg korba*) 72

Sándor Reményik

THE CHURCH AND THE SCHOOL (*Templom és iskola*) 73
THE DESERTER LILY BLOOM (*Elpártolt liliomszál*) 75
ANY WAY YOU CAN (*Ahogy lehet*) 76
THE HUNGARIAN TRICOLOR (*Három szín*) 78

Árpád Tóth

YOU DROPPED THE SUN (*Elejtetted a napot*) 79
EEVENING SUNRAY WREATH (*From "Esti sugárkoszorú"*) 81

INTERWAR YEARS (1920-1940)

Lajos Kassák

A WORKER PORTRAIT (*Munkásportré*) 85
THE ENFORCEMENT OF THE LAW (*A törvény végrehajtása*) 86
MAYEM AT NIGHT (*Az éjszaka zűrzavara*) 88
BEFORE MY PAINTINGS (*Festményeim előtt*) 89
THE END OF THE LEGEND (*A legenda vége*) 90

Attila József

THE SONG OF A GRIEVING HUNGARIAN (*Bús magyar éneke*) 91
WITH A PURE HEART (*Tiszta szívvel*) 92
MY MOTHER (*Anyám*) 93
MAMA (*Mama*) 94
I'LL BE A GARDENER (*Kertész leszek*) 95
IF YOU DON'T... (*Ha nem szorítasz...*) 96
THE POOR ARE THE POOREST (*Aki szegény, az a legszegényebb*) 97
MY HOMELAND (*Hazám*) 98
PROFIT (*Haszon*) 99
IT'S NOT ME YELLING (*Nem én kiáltok*) 100
CHRISTMAS (*Karácsony*) 101
FOR MY BIRTHDAY (*Születésnapomra*) 102
GOD (*Isten*) 104
NO ONE WILL HELP ME UP (*Nem emel fel*) 105

Jenő Dsida

HYMN TO SNOWFALLS TO COME (Jövendő havak himnusza) 106
NOCTURNAL VISIT (Éji látogatás) 107
TWILIGHT (Alkony) 108
NOTHING'S DREAM (A Semmi álma) 109
SHADOW ON THE WALL (Árnyék a falon) 110
THE LAST OUR FATHER (Az utolsó Miatyánk) 111

Lőrinc Szabó

CYANIDE, HANDGUN (*Méreg, revolver*) 112
WILD WEST EUROPE (*Wild West Európa*) 113
HOUSES, PALACES, BALDHEADED THIEVES (*Házak, paloták, kopasz bűnösök*) 114
THERE'S NO MONEY AND WE MUST EAT (*Nincs pénz és enni kell*) 115
EXPLOSIONS (*Robbanások*) 117
LOUNGING AMONG FLOWERS (*Virágok közt hevertünk*) 118
SINCE YOU'RE NOWHERE (*Mert sehol se vagy*) 119

YOU'RE EVERYWHERE (*Mindenütt ott vagy*) 120
NOTHING ELSE (*Egyéb nem*) 121

WARS OF DISTOPIAS (1939-1956)

Miklós Radnóti

NO WAY OF KNOWING... (*Nem tudhatom...*) 125
THE FUGITIVE (*A bujdosó*) 127
RAZGLEDNICAS (*Razglednicák*) 128

Sándor Márai

EPILOGUE (*Utóirat*) 130
ANGEL FROM HEAVEN (*Mennyből az angyal*) 131

Gyula Illyés

TYRANNY IN ONE SENTENCE (Egy mondat a zsarnokságról) 134

György Faludy

FAREWELL TO RECSK (*Búcsú Recsktől*) 140
LOVE SONNET (S. 21) (*Hol válik el, S.21*) 141

WAITING FOR THE NEXT (1945-1990)

Sándor Weöres

GOLDEN CORD (*Aranyzsinór*) 145
SUNKEN SIGNS (*Elsüllyedt jelek*) 145
THE RIDER OF THE PLAZA (*A tér lovasa*) 146
LIGHTS GONE OUT (*Kialudt fények*) 147
AFTER CREATION (*A teremtés után*) 148
THE WORLD OF ENNUI (*Az unalmas világ*) 149

János Pilinszky

THE ANGEL OF BRIGHTNESS (*A fennséges angyal*) 150

FABULA (*Fable*) 151

KNOCKING (*Kopogtatnak*) 152

László Nagy

FIRE (*Tűz*) 153

WHO CAN FERRY LOVE ACROSS (*Ki viszi át a Szerelmet*) 154

Sándor Kányádi

BEHIND GOD'S BACK (*Isten háta mögött*) 155

MISMATCHED AUTUMN LOVESONG (*Felemás őszi ének*) 156

Gizella Hervay

NAKED BEFORE INTERROGATION LIGHTS (*Meztelenül a vallatófényben*) 157

DEFENSELESS (*Védtelenül*) 158

THE GUARDIAN (*Vigyázó*) 159

SPRING (*Tavasz*) 159

RESUME (*Űrlap*) 160

Appendix

POSTSCRIPT 163

A POET'S COMMENTS ON PILLARS OF MAGYAR POETRY 165

ACKNOWLEDGEMENTS 169

ABOUT THE TRANSLATOR 171

PILLARS OF MAGYAR POETRY

Hungarian poems selected and translated by Paul Sohar

FOREWARD

The title of this book is not sufficiently generous; Hungarian poets have been the pillars of not only Magyar (Hungarian) poetry but also that of national survival as well. Just look at this collection of poems I have more or less randomly put together; some of them were translated on request, some appealed to my own poetic inclination while others just happened to demand my attention because they played a significant role in Hungarian history by giving voice to the people of Hungary in critical situations. Some of them not only reflected historical events but instigated them. Nowhere is that role better advocated than in a stanza of the poem "To Nineteenth-Century Poets" (*A XIX-ik század költőihez*) by Sándor Petőfi, Hungary's national poet:

> Let no one engage in plucking strings
> with idle hands, just to pass the time!
> It is a heavy task these days
> to endow those strings with rhyme.
> If you can't sing about anything else
> but your private joy or ire,
> the world has no more use for you.
> Set aside the holy lyre.

To my knowledge such a command was never issued with such force and clarity to the poets of Western Europe, where the purview of poetry was traditionally left outside of social concerns. This was a privilege enjoyed in the relatively peaceful parts of the Continent but unfortunately, not given to the Eastern parts, especially not to Hungary. Admittedly, Hungarians were initially responsible for the disturbance of the peace when they pushed their way into the Carpathian Basin, if indeed there was peace in that area at that time, in the Ninth Century. This was the time of the Dark Ages, and the people living in that conquered territory didn't write their own history, they left it to Byzantine scribes. Hungary as a state was established in the year 1000 A.D. when the son of the chosen high chief of the seven Hungarian tribes was crowned as the King of Hungary under the name of Steven (István in Hungarian, Stephanus in Latin, the language of the Church, and later sainted to Saint Steven), Hungary prospered and developed as a European nation imbued with Christian culture over the next 500 years with one short but devastating interruption when the Mongols occupied and plundered the country for one year in the early thirteenth century, Not only was the majority of the population killed off but all written documents and newly erected gothic structures were demolished. In the following three hundred years Hungary slowly recovered and even thrived until the middle of the sixteenths century when there was a Muslim invasion with equal result, except it lasted 150 years instead of just one. Hungary has never been an independent nation since then. Unfortunately, the result is only too simple to describe: the area that comprises the present state of Hungary was under Turkish rule and more or less totally destroyed, and Hungary survived only in the areas that are no longer part of Hungary, if that makes any sense. What happened was that at the end of seventeenth century the combined forces of Western European nations reconquered Hungary and put it under the rule of the Habsburg Empire of Austria. In 1848 there was an uprising against the Austrian domination, at which time Petőfi, a young firebrand poet, called upon his fellow Hungarian poets to answer the call and join the revolution—not only with a sword but the pen as well. In addition, he called for a social revolution added to the fight for national liberation as demonstrated by this fragment from his poem "String Up All the Kings!" (*Akasszátok fel a királyokat!*), a stirring call for the abolition of the feudalist system and its political powerhead, the monarchy.

Haven't you people learned this one key thing,
To wholeheartedly hate your pompous king?
I so much wish I could only disseminate
Amongst you this wild and reckless hate
That my breast, like a swelling ocean, brings!
Go you poor serfs, string up all the kings!

Every part in his heart is filled with doom,
He brings evil from his mother's womb,
His whole life is a sinful, wicked wrack,
Wherever he looks the air turns black,
Where he's buried the soil spoils and stinks—
Go you people, string up all the kings!

Give pardon and friendship to everyone,
But to kings that must never be done!
I shall toss my pen and lyre aside,
And take the hangman's job in stride
If no one else can bother with such things—
Come on folks, let's string up all the kings!

With the help of the Russian Tsar the struggle for independence was suppressed and Hungary remained under Austrian rule until after the disastrous First World War when Hungary became a separate kingdom but without a king and without all the areas that had preserved Hungarian identity during the Turkish rule; the country was reduced to one-third of its original size in the Paris Peace Treaty—which will be depicted in several poems of this collection. Things only got worse later on in the twentieth century; the interwar years were marked by the Great Depression, followed by World War II., a horror that subjected Hungary to oppression by two equally deadly ideologies, Nazism and Soviet communism. Poets responded to all these upheavals in their works; that is why it is important to keep the historical background in mind. Even personal poems, love poems, nature poems, all are overshadowed or colored by social conditions.

The reader may ask why the preponderance of twentieth century poets? Were there no poets in the nineteenth century to answer Petőfi's call? The answer is simply exigency, the availability of this translator's works. Some of them already published in literary journals, some even in books, but all of them just lying around and waiting to see the light of day. Only one poem was translated especially for this collection, Balassi's poem celebrating the troops, especially the cavalry, defending the tenuous frontline during the Turkish occupation in the sixteenth century. He was essentially the first poet to choose the vernacular to write his poems; before him poetry had been written in Latin, the language of learning and culture.

Perhaps it was not by accident that the first Hungarian poet was also a warrior and that the latter role was foisted upon him. The turbulent history of his country is defined by a series of wars, all calamitous for the country; it's a miracle that the country still exists. Therefore, it seemed only natural that its literary development be divided into periods separated by wars.

Another thing that may puzzle the reader is why choose a nineteenth century poet, Petőfi, to speak for the translator when the book is filled with twentieth century poets? The answer is simple: the issues back then seemed to be more clear-cut, untainted by misleading ideological slogans, and Petőfi had no trouble finding the right words to define them. In addition, up until his time, poetry had not been pursued in so many divergent styles as later. Nobody had any trouble understanding what Petőfi stood for; on the contrary, everybody was carried away by the stormy wind of his stanzas. And Petőfi's poetry, like good wine, has even increased its potency with time.

Besides being limited to poets who are no longer with us, the capricious nature of this selection of twentieth century poets is only partly due to the fact that it concentrated on my personal favorites; in addition, some of the best-known ones (Faludy, Kányádi, Szőcs, Farkas Arpád) have already received a whole book of translation from me. The other glaring gaps in my translation oeuvre are waiting for my future attention; there are many more favorites. (Many more than the years I have left.) In general though, each era of the last century is represented by a few poems that have made a place for themselves among the timeless masterpieces of Hungarian poetry, here called by its true name, Magyar poetry, just to add a little flavor of the culture.

A few biographical notes about the poets in order of their presentation in this selection for the better appreciation of their works:

Bálint Balassi (1554-1594), born into a landholding noble family, he came with knighthood already bestowed upon him yet he pursued it with great zest, ultimately to his detriment; in one of the skirmishes with the occupying Muslim forces he suffered a fatal wound. Luckily though, he found enough time for poetry to such an extent that he was given a post as a teacher of that art. Too bad he could not resist the call of battlefield glory.

Mihály Csokonai (1773-1805) was born to more modest circumstances and led a more peaceful life as a private tutor to aristocratic families. The adventure in his life was his association with traveling theater companies as a playwright, specializing in comedies. There is no war heard in the background, only rococo sentiments in abundance.

Sándor Petőfi (1823-1849) was the son of a village tavern keeper, but in his short life he managed to rise to the position of the number one poet of Hungary, especially in lyric style. He died or disappeared as a civilian reporter under unclear circumstances in the last battle of Hungary's fight for freedom from the Habsburg Empire. He is still considered the national poet of Hungary yet, at the same time, he personifies the ability of Magyar culture to unify disparate ethnicities; he was born with the Serbian name of Alexander Petrovics.

János Arany (1817-1882) lived a less adventurous life as a journalist and poet. He did not compete with his friend Petőfi, a better-known contemporary in lyric poetry, but he excelled in ballads. His Shakespeare translations can still be heard in Hungarian theaters.

Endre Ady (1877-1919, Hungary), made a breakthrough in Hungarian poetry when he filled formal verse with contemporary language and contents, while fighting the vestiges of feudalism at the turn of the century. He simply called his first book *New Poems* (1906); his last book (*Leading the Dead*, 1918) contains anti-war poems, protesting The Great War from the very beginning; the eponymous poem is in this selection.

Dezső Kosztolányi (1885-1936) also broke with the style of the nineteenth century and was an editor of *Nyugat* (West), the most influential literary journal featuring the modern tendencies taking over Western Europe.

Mihály Babits (1983-1941) was also a supporter of the "urban" trends in culture as opposed to the "populists" who cultivated the native culture at that time. His warning against Nazi takeover is still often quoted: "If you stay silent among murderers, you become one of them."

Sándor Reményik (1890-1941) was a native of Transylvania, a part of Hungary that was taken away from Hungary in the Paris Peace Treaty after the Great War and given to Romania. He used his poetry to fight for the return of this Hungarian province to Hungary.

Árpád Tóth (1886-1942) a lyric poet who was best known for his translations of poetry, an important accomplishment in a small country where at least half of all published literature comes from abroad compared to 4% in Anglophone countries.

Lajos Kassák (1887-1962) came from a poor background but with a quick mind that embraced modern developments not only in literature (Dada) and art (abstract constructivism) but politics as well and briefly served as member of the short-lived communist government in 1919. But rebels do not tolerate rebels among themselves, and he remained an outsider even after WWII, when the invading Soviets installed a more permanent communist system.

Attila József (1905-1937) also grew up in truly poor, proletarian circumstances without a father and losing his mother while still a minor, becoming his sister's ward. For his "With a Pure Heart" poem he was dismissed from the university, never to finish his formal education but still achieve recognition for his poetry; nevertheless, he died an early death of suicide.

Jenő Dsida (1907-1938) also died young but of natural causes; his very inventive free verse was still far ahead of his time.

Lőrinc Szabó (1900-1957) is best known now for his lyrical love poems in sonnet form, but some of his early free verse compares well with the rebellious tone of his more proletarian colleagues.

Miklós Radnóti (1909-1944) was a teacher by profession, but as a Jew he had to serve in a work brigade during WWII and died during its last months in retreat. After the war his body was found with his last poems ("Razglednicas") still in his pocket.

Sándor Márai (1900-1989) had a very successful international career as a novelist and dramatist in the interwar years in addition to being a poet. The two poems in this anthology very heart-wrenchingly record two historic tragedies in Hungary, the destructive siege of Budapest in 1944 and the Uprising in 1956.

Gyula Illyés (1902-1983) was better known as novelist than a poet; his description of the poor peasant life in the 30s established his reputation as a populist writer even though he spent several years in Paris in the company of the luminaries of French literature. His long poem here about the Stalinist style tyranny introduced into Hungary after WWII was only known through samizdat literature until after his death.

György Faludy (1910-2006) made an early reputation for himself with his Villon translations and imitations. He spent most of WWII in the US serving in the Army, but as an ardent socialist he went back to Hungary to help build socialism after the war. But in 1948 the Communist Party took complete control of the government by taking over the Party of the Social Democrats, imprisoning its uncooperative leaders and prominent supporters. Faludy was placed in a Soviet-style gulag, a work camp whose main purpose was to starve the inmates to death. After Stalin's death, these camps were dismantled, and Faludy got to write about his experiences in some of his best poems. The complete collection if his prison poems are in my Faludy book: *Silver Pirouettes* (Ragged Sky Press, 2016)

Sándor Weöres (1913-1989) was the first contemporary poet I discovered on my own as a teenager in a journal *Diarium*. Later it turned out that indeed he had made a permanent place for himself in Hungarian literature.

János Pilinszky (1921-1981) is perhaps the second best-known Hungarian poet in the Anglophone areas besides Attila József.

László Nagy (1925-1978); on returning to my homeland on visits after a long hiatus, I found Nagy to be my favorite among the new names always present in the yearly anthologies of contemporary poets.

Sándor Kányádi (1929-2018) is a towering figure among the Transylvanian-Hungarian poets who successfully experimented in modern styles as well as with traditional forms with modern language and vivid images. My translation volume *In Contemporary Tense* contains an extensive (almost comprehensive) selection of his poetry. We had several joint bilingual readings together in Hungary and twice traveled all the way to Prague for such occasions.

Gizella Hervay (1934-1982) is not included here just to represent female poets but as a poet who represents the best in modern poetry. She was born in Hungary but moved to Transylvania and married Domokos Szilágyi, a famous poet there, but after he and the son died, both under separate tragic circumstances, she moved to Budapest where she worked as a journalist until she also took her own life. Her poems reflect the intensity of her life in bold, modernistic style.

WARS OF OLD

Bálint Balassi

SOLDIER SONG IN PRAISE OF THE FRONTLINES
(*Egy katonaének; in laudem confiniorum*)

You frontier knights, what could be as fine as guarding frontline forts?
There, at dawn, a choir of fair birds sings; they share with us their course,
The field grants us scent, the sky drops dew; couldn't get more by force.

The news of enemy often makes a soldier's heart start beating fast,
Even without it these guardians of the line ride off for fun at last,
To kill, capture, fight, and to get wounded with blood on their faces cast.

Under crimson flags these soldiers, bearing their festooned spears to wield
Before the vast enemy horde, go riding forth to reconnoiter the field;
All dressed in leopard mantles, on their shakos fancy plumes are sealed.

Under them Arabian horses prance, impatient at the trumpet sound,
The knight on guard dismounts and takes his rest with sun around
The others at night, exhausted from battles, sleep well on the ground.

For fame, good name and lasting honor they leave the world without a care,
They set the example of knighthood and its pledge of always being fair;
But like hawks they scour the field, slashing to let the rivals have their share.

Spying enemy, they shout with joy as they go and break many a spear;
If things get tough in the fray, without being called, on duty they appear,
Although even bloodied, they can turn on their pursuers without much fear.

The big wide field and the forest shade is their castle for a pleasant stroll,
The roadside ambush and the battlefield is the school where they enroll;
Hunger in long battle, thirst in the heat of it, and fatigue are food for the soul.

They take pleasure in the sharpness of the saber because their job is to behead,
On the fields of conflict many of them are lying wounded, many of them dead,
Their corpses finding grave in the bellies of carrion birds or beasts instead.

Oh, you guardians of frontlines, the highly praised band of sapling knights,
Whose good name has gotten around the world for your fearless fights;
Like trees with fruit, may God bless you in the field with fortune's rights.

Mihály Csokonai

TO HOPE

(*Reményhez*)

A mirage made in the sky
Toying with mortals down here,
The hope we worship on the sly
Will tease us just to disappear.
A god the unhappy man
Creates for himself,
A guardian angel he can
Forever beg for help.
Why lure me with smooth lips?
Why keep smiling my way?
Why keep forcing bogus drips
Of spirit in this tired clay?
Get going! You're a curse!
You promised me a crown;
I fell for the saccharine words,
But you let me down.

You planted daffodils
In all my garden nooks;
You watered all my trees
With gently babbling brooks;
You bathed me in springtide
With a thousand flowers
And with joy you spiced
My waking blinks and hours.
My morning thoughts as they rose
All headed like a busy bee
For my beloved rose
With whom they longed to be.
From my happiness barred
Was only one last bit:
I prayed for Lilla's heart,
And Heaven granted it.

But then my rosy greenery
Began to wither away;
My spring and every tree
Dried up one gloomy day;
My springtime merriment
Turned to winter blues;
My world came to an end
In another's foul use.
Only if my loved one
Had been left to me
I wouldn't wail so wan
About this calamity.
In her arms I could forget
All my present woes;
From me success has fled,
Who cares to whom it goes!

Leave me, hope, alone and still!
I know the reality
Of my misfortune will
Tomorrow surely bury me.
In my despair I feel
My former spirit wane,
It's Heaven my soul seeks
And my body the grave.
Bloomless are the meadows,
The field a vacant site,
In the grove silence grows,
The sun sinks into night.
Charming, mellow trillas!
Mirages in the sky!
Hope! High spirits! Lillas!
To you all, I say goodbye!

Mihály Csokonai

HESITANT REQUEST
(*Tartozkodó kérelem*)

A mighty love burns up my calm,
Devours me through and through.
For this you could be the balm,
You lovely little tulip, you.

In your eyes a daybreak
Lights up a lively fire,
Your dewy lips could make
a thousand cares expire.

Grant your lover what he misses
With an angelic sigh:
With a thousand fervent kisses
I'll reward your sweet reply.

LETHE

Where are they, Lethe's relaxing shores,
The quiet, know-nothing, feel-nothing bliss?
Which corner of earth hides that happy land
Where science and headache don't mix,
Where the sweetest sensation is its lack,
Where forgetfulness lets you hit the sack?
A grove inhabited by ambling shades
Where humans as humans are born again.
You blessed land, after death you erase all
Memories no matter how long a life we gain,
Take pity on me and take in my soul
Before I must finish playing this mortal role.

Sándor Petőfi

NATIONAL CALL
(*Nemzeti dal*)

Rise you Magyars, heed the call!
It's now or never, do not stall!
Shall we live enslaved or free?
Choose your chains or liberty.
  On the God of Hungary
  We swear,
  We swear,
  No more chains for us to bear!

Too long we have been prisoners,
The victims of an evil curse.
Our forebears lived and died unbound,
They cannot rest in servile ground.
  On the God of Hungary
  We swear,
  We swear,
  No more chains for us to bear!

Only a knave is too afraid
To perish in his country's aid
And values his wretched life above
His homeland's honor and its love.
  On the God of Hungary
  We swear,
  We swear,
  No more chains for us to bear!

The sword is brighter than the chain,
The arm looks better in its flame.
Then why the shackles tied on fast?
Let us grab our swords at last!
  On the God of Hungary

We swear,
We swear,
No more chains for us to bear!

Hungary will shine again,
Worthy of its golden name,
We shall wash it clean of dirt
Smeared on it by years' of hurt!
On the God of Hungary
We swear,
We swear,
No more chains for us to bear!

In our graveyard on a hill,
On their knees our children will
Bless our tombstones and declaim
On them every holy name.
On the God of Hungary
We swear,
We swear,
No more chains for us to bear!

[*This poem, written in March 1848 and recited by the poet at public gatherings, ignited a revolution against the Hapsburg rule over Hungary.*]

Sándor Petőfi

MY WINTER IN DEBRECZEN
(*Egy telem Debreczenben*)

Hey, you, town of Debreczen,
how often you taunt my mind
with the suffering you gave to me!...
And yet you remain
a beloved and kind
old guest in my memory.

A papist I am surely not,
yet I fasted there a lot.
Good thing the gods made mortal teeth
out of bone by wise design. No doubt,
had my teeth been made of steel,
they would've surely rusted out.

In the middle of a raw
winter of snow and sleet
my stove ran out of straw
and I slept without a whiff of heat.
Putting on my worn-out set
of rags I could easily recite
with the gypsy caught in a net:
"Must be real cold outside!"

The only help to me
was my poetry!
But how to record my riff
with fingers frozen stiff?
At last, I hit upon the very thing,
kept my fingers twisted tight
around my always burning pipe,
till the welcome breeze of spring.

One thought got me through the fast:
I'd fasted much worse in the past.

1843

Sándor Petőfi

SEPTEMBER

(*Szeptember*)

Fall is here again and its
Beauty gets me every time,
All I know is that I love it
Without a reason or a rhyme.

Sitting on a lonely hill
I let the landscape come to me,
And listen to the falling leaves
Playing their soft symphony.

LIBERTY AND LOVE

(*Szabadság, szerelem...*)

Liberty and love.
These two are dear to me;
I'd give up my life for love,
And my love for liberty!

János Arany

THE WORLD
(A világ)

This world is now a rundown cart,
Still can move, but not too far;
It's broken there and ripped right here:
Won't abduct you, don't you fear.

The world is now a tattered cape,
Moth-eaten, moldy, and frayed,
Spots fall off, holes too big to mend:
Thread can only speed the end.

The world is a lakeside watermill;
Sometimes an ocean to the fill,
Sometimes not a drop, as dry as dirt;
When it's needed, it doesn't work.

The world is an old musician
Without a smidgen of ambition;
It's only half a note he can play,
Forgets a new song every day.

The world is a broken-down saloon,
A poor place in January or June;
In winter too cold, in summer too wet,
Yet you sit there every chance you get.

The world is just a helpless drunk:
In his own tracks he gets sunk;
Wants to leap over hill and dale,
It's the level ground he cannot scale.

THE ANCIENT TOWER

(*Az ó torony*)

Nagy-Szalonta is a famous city,
Now less famous and more gritty,
Not like when it was a rebel fort;
Three hundred stayed there in its fold.

A crumbling tower scrapes the cloudy sky,
That's where the setting sun likes to lie:
I see my forebears' blood in the way
It splashes on the wall its last red ray.

Why does it send that blood-red glow?
Does it mean a bad day for tomorrow?
We've had many a bad day before,
My God, with ice and snow galore!

Even in this godforsaken place,
How many hearts once bled with grace!
They said they had their homeland to defend,
Believing they could stave off its end.

And what is left of their sacrifice?...
The tower that they managed to devise.
Like a Babel, the tower is still stark,
Time has passed it without a mark.

On top of it a stork's leg bends,
Jays and owls are steady residents.
Even pigeons make a home in here,
Assimilate slowly without much fear.

Wild weeds amass a garden there,
The wind and they tear each other's hair.
It can even take the heavy jolt
Given by the mace of a thunder bolt.

On stormy nights its crumbling wall
Accommodates a noisy witches' ball.
The next day its signs are easily found
In the stones kicked off to the ground.

János Arany

SHIPWRECKED
(*A hajótörött*)

When the waves still perceived
Signs of life in his floppy limbs
They took the last remaining
Wooden board away from him;
When at last they thought him dead
They refused him a graveyard plot,
Tossing him on a ragged shore:
Let the dirt there seal his lot.
        Fear the wrath of God, you people!
        Cries the shipwrecked sailor there;
        Give him shelter and refuge,
        Some food and warm clothes to wear.

Only yesterday so many ships
Were bearing treasures galore,
Millions were hauling untold
Millions and much more:
Not the tears of orphans and
Sad widows, not a stolen hoard,
But the pearls that persistence
And perspiration would afford.
        Fear the wrath of God, you people!
        Worldly goods are not here to stay;
        Tomorrow may not see the stuffed
        Chests or the ships so full today.

Yesterday he still believed
His life was safely in his hands
And his old age beckoned to him
From the safety of sunny lands;
He'd done the right accounting,
Accounting for all, more or less,
He had no reason at the end
To fear that last big zero: death.

Fear the wrath of God, you people!
Life's accounting is relative:
A heart bereft of hope would die,
But as a beggar he must live.

János Arany

AT HOME

(*Itthon*)

Like a fowl for its nest,
A thirsty hiker for a stream,
A child for his mother's lap,
I yearn for this lovely scene.

At home among my loved ones
My loving world waits for me;
It may be overcast outside:
Here there are always stars to see.

Starry eyes, lips about to smile:
This is what my heart desires,
And stepping over the threshold
This is what my heart admires.

My heart renews itself, a child,
Whose small joys it magnifies,
I'm surrounded by the spirit
Of playful, harmless butterflies.

For a while I can let go of
My cares about the coming day:
And shed the weight off my shoulders,
Lest it turn joy to dismay.

With child heart, unconsciously
I rest easy thinking this:
He who's the father of us all
Will not forsake those who are his.

János Arany

MY HOPE

(Reményem)

1.
My hope is but a tiny boat
Without a rudder or a mast;
The restless breakers toss it hard,
To and fro they let it cast.
2.
The blue shore is far behind.
From the barren land of reality
Into self-exile this vain
Little boat, my hope, ferries me.
3.
Like a swan that ran away
To hide out on the high seas;
Knocked by one wave to the next,
A safe haven is not what it seeks.
4.
My soul, the sailor of the ocean,
Afraid of pulling to a pier
Where the thorns hide no roses
And the dust lets no blooms appear.
5.
Where the ground is hard and solid
So that those still hunting me
Can follow my tracks in this field
More bravely and more easily.
6.
Away then, into the unknown now!
When I'm driven by wind and crest:
I feel a relief from my tortures
When by wind and surf possessed.

7.
Out there I can breathe more freely,
Sometimes even a rainbow might
Smile at me, though wrecked I am
On the ocean of my inner sight.

8.
Away, away, into the unknown now!
You, my boat, just ride the open seas!
Let me forget running like this
Where death begins and dreams must cease.

TRIAL BY THE CORPSE

(*Tetemre hivás*)

In the deep dark forest of Radvány
Was Bárczy Benő discovered dead.
A spiky dagger in his youthful heart:
"Here's the evidence and it's easily read:
Violence caused his blood to be shed."

His father had him brought into the fort
And on cold stone floor placed on display
Without him having been washed and dressed:
Frozen in blood as found, he lies at rest
On this bier uncovered day after day.

Four guardsmen are posted nearby:
"Not a soul's allowed in or out..."
"What if his mother and sister come and try
To mourn him?" – "Turn them back;
These orders are for no one to flout!"

From hall to hidden hall, choking force
And silent sobs of womanly woe at loose. –
Let the law issue "summons to the corpse"
To whoever bears the shadow of doubt:
Let the bleeding of the wound accuse.

The palace is wrapped in black drapery,
Even at noon the sun can't reach its walls;
The corpse is surrounded by courtroom props,
Candle, crucifix, canonized priests and cops:
Wax yellow light on the funeral palls.

"Summon his enemies, if any indeed!"
They enter, all those the father can name;
In vain! The wound doesn't open to bleed
Faced by anyone, the result is the same:
"Not guilty...." again there's no one to blame.

"Then who did it?..." Bárczi's cry is dark and raw,
"It is revenge this ancient blood demands;
Get that murderer! ... even if my thirst for law
Should pierce my heart with the fateful charge:
Everyone's a suspect, everyone alive who stands!"

"Summon his young friends, all of them!"
One after another they duly appear:
It hurts them to see the hero frozen in blood
Instead of falling in a battlefield flood.
But there's no bleeding fresh on the bier.

"Summon the whole household! All of them!...
Summon the entire village of Bárcz!"
Tears flood the eyes of all the women and men,
They look at their dear lord with heavy hearts.
But no bleeding from the wound ever starts.

"Summon his mother! His unwed sister!"
Already outside the girl begins to scream;
The mother slumps down on him squealing:
But the dead displays no sign of feeling:
His blood remains a black spot, not a stream.

"Summon at last his beautiful beloved,
His secret betrothed, the Kunds' Abigail!"
She enters; - her eyes flash, then on the dagger land,
Her face a mask, her feet root where they stand.
- The blood's gushing red this time and doesn't fail.

No tears are running, no scream from her,
Just her hands fly to her head, the source of truth:
Horror inside her slowly begins to stir!...
The heart skips beating on hearing the charge:
"My girl, you are the murderer of this youth!"

As the blood's witness is rightly confirmed
She's silent -enthralled - then her voice comes alive:
"It was not I who killed Bárczi Benő, I swear,
Heaven be my witness and the angels up there!
However, it was I who gave him the knife.

My heart belonged to him in eternal love -
He knew of nothing to keep us apart:
Yet he pestered me for a verbal "yes",
If it's a "no", he said it'll be his death.
I laughed: see if this dagger finds your heart!"

From the wound wrenching the dagger the maid
Sets her eyes shooting out terrible flares,
Laughing and crying she flashes the blade
And runs off with the screech of a jay.
To lay a hand on her no one dares.

Outside she gambols and runs in the street,
Dancing and singing in front of the house;
"Once there was girl who used to enjoy
Playing with her adoring lover boy
Like a cat is wont to do with a mouse."

CIVILIZATION
(*Civilizáció*)

In early times, wars were fought
without a sanction or excuse.
The strong simply had to grab
what they wanted for their use.

Not so now. The world is run
by meetings, not by brute force.
Pranks done by the strong are things
to debate and then endorse.

1877

WARS OF DECLINE

ON NEW WATERS I SAIL

(*Új vizeken járok*)

Have no fear, my ship, tomorrow is on board,
The jeering mob can't keep this drunken oarsman moored.
Ride the waves, my ship,
Have no fear, my ship: tomorrow is on board.

To go on flying, flying on and on and on
To great new Waters, virgin Waters, like a swan,
Ride the waves, my ship,
To go on flying, flying on and on and on.

New horizons are arising to caress your eyes,
Every minute mounts a whole new Paradise,
Ride the waves, my ship,
New horizons are arising to caress your eyes.

To hell with all old rancid dreams already dreamt,
On waves of new pains, secrets, and thirsts I'm sent,
Ride the waves, my ship,
To hell with all old rancid dreams already dreamt.

I'll never be a fiddler of the marketplace,
Whether driven by wine or a holy face:
Ride the waves, my ship,
I'll never be a fiddler of the marketplace.

1907

Endre Ady

THE LADY OF THE CASTLE IN WHITE
(*A vár fehér asszonya*)

Within me looms a heathen castle,
Adorned with haughty moss and woe.
(My eyes, you see how wide they are?
And how dead their glow, how dead their glow.)

The empty halls hold hollow echoes,
And glaring from the baleful walls
Are two huge windows toward the valley.
(Aren't these eyes spent cannonballs?)

The haunting here is unrelieved,
The reek of crypts cements the mist,
Mute shadows shamble through the darkness,
Their scars by curse-crossed armies hissed.

(A rare and secret midnight hour
May set these gloomy eyes aglow.)
The castle's white-frocked lady strolls by
The windows with a laugh to throw.

Endre Ady

WHEN THE PYRE DIES

(*Hunyhat a máglya*)

These sad, sepulchral eyes
Shall never stare at someone else's
When the pyre dies.

Banish me you may,
But from these faithful, old, dog-eyes
You'll never tear yourself away.

A new adventure might again
Ignite your heartbeat's pyre:
But all in vain, but all in vain.

Their horror maybe hit you hard:
With these faithful eyes on duty,
All escape routes will be barred.

Endre Ady

MATING ON THE AUTUMN LEAVES

(*Héja-nász az avaron*)

We take off, migrate into Fall,
A screeching, weeping game's our brawl,
A buzzard pair with flagging wings.

New bandits plunder Summer's heat,
Their wings clank out a mortal beat,
Embraces' mangling clashes rage.

We wing our way from Summer, chased,
In Fall we seek rest from love's haste,
Our feathers frightened, still in love.

Tonight's the final wedding night:
In our flesh our claws delight,
Then down we drop on autumn leaves.

Endre Ady

LEDA'S HEART
(A Léda szíve)

A witches' gaggle pelted me
With fear to which I did not hark
In somber wonders' shrill amusement park,
Although my lover took to flight,
My fair lost lover: youthful Smile.

*

The witches wept and laughed around me.
The mournful fog was dusty dark
In somber wonders' dim amusement park.
Against a rain of hearts, I had
To raise my hands to shield my face.

*

With hearts the witches pelted me
and fear to which I did not hark.
In somber wonders' grim amusement park
I stood alone there and forlorn.
The fog sent down a rain of hearts,
Unyielding, ugly, little hearts.

*

Then suddenly the witches parted for
A cloud of tearful whiteness in the dark
In somber wonders' grim amusement park
A woman dressed in rays of light appeared,
And toward that light I turned my face.

*

She looked me in the eye, reaching in her chest;
On my face I still can feel her mark.
In somber wonders' shrill amusement park
Into my face she flung her heart,
Her warmish, sickly, wretched heart.

ON THE SHORES OF THE BLUE SEA

(*A kék tenger partján*)

Where others live and love in peace
I'm driven by an old disease
To sink a kiss, a cast-off dream,
And serenity on shores serene.

Tomorrow holds for me a home,
Not the place where now I roam,
I yearned to come here but can't stay.
A ghost I am, sick, sad, and fey.

THE BLACK-LACQUERED CONCERT GRAND

(*A fekete zongora*)

Its crazy nerve-strings boom and whine
A song the wineless cannot stand:
The black-lacquered concert grand.
Its blind maestro dives with glee
Inside to forge life's melody:
The black-lacquered concert grand.

The buzz within, my teardrop eyes, where
Deranged desires' banquets land,
All that and more: the concert grand.
To this mad beat my heart now spews
Its blood out to be filled with booze:
This is the black concert grand.

Endre Ady

TO WEEP AND WEEP

(Sírni, sírni, sírni)

To watch for an approaching coffin
While the clock strikes twelve at night.

To toll the bells without asking
Who's buried in the funeral rite.

To dangle a mourning crucifix
In a black tent filled with smoke,

To dress in black and weighty silver,
Holding flares until we choke.

To start a fight with rattling shadows,
To chant in strains a strangled hymn.

To soak in the roar of organs and
Sepulchral voices from within.

To stumble over deep open graves
Behind glum priests and altar boys.

To go on secret spying missions
To catch a glimpse of a stranger's corpse.

To shiver in a mystic moonlit night
In incense mist that makes you wheeze.

To deny the past and beat your breast
In mystic ecstasy on your knees.

To atone for all and fall down broken
On a nameless coffin in a heap.

To write a testament, a frightful one,
And then just weep and weep and weep.

Endre Ady

THE COUSIN OF DEATH

(*A Halál rokona*)

I am the Cousin of Death,
waning loves can claim my heart,
I love to kiss those preparing
to depart.

I love pale, sickly roses,
women wilting from desire,
slanted sunrays, sad autumn days
about to expire.

I love the ghostly beckoning
of sorrowful, long hours,
the playful mimicry of sacred Death,
and Death's great flowers.

I love those departing,
those who weep on awakening
on meadows at dawn when cold
frost showers sing.

I love languid resignation,
tearless crying and its peace,
the refuge of thinkers, poets
and the ill in release.

I love the disappointed,
the crippled with maladies,
those bereft of hope and beliefs:
I love the world as it is.

I am the cousin of Death,
I love the love that's losing heart,
I love to kiss the beloved friend
about to depart

MY BRIDE

(*Az én menyasszonyom*)

What do I care if she's a street-corner slave
as long as she sees me off all the way to the grave.

Let her stand in broiling summer heat before
me saying: "It's you I love, it's you I've been waiting for."

Let her be a slut, kicked out from home in disgrace
as long as in her heart I can claim a place.

When we stand in a wild storm and swear:
let us break our legs and collapse together there.

When our souls get recharged in an hour:
let us find joy in each other's lips we devour.

If I fall down and roll around in the dust of the road:
let her fall on me, hugging me in a protective mode.

If I am fired up by a purifying holy flame:
let us wing our way over the world, it'll be ours to claim.

Let her shower me with kisses and love all the time:
even in dirt, in tears, in suffering and grime.

When I fail my dreams and they fail to arrive,
let her retrieve them: let Her be Life.

In her gaudy make-up I detect an angel face:
Her soul would be my soul: my life and death.

Crushing every stone tablet and every iron chain,
we'd be laughing at the world to the last breath.

We'd be laughing while waving final farewell
and die together deifying each other by the knell.

We'd die proclaiming what we know:
"Life is but sin and dirt,
only two of us were pure, as pure as falling snow."

Endre Ady

THE SONG OF A CHEERFUL FUNERAL
(*Vidám temetés éneke*)

Things that pass away turn ugly fast,
even sorrow loses beauty when it's gone,
that's why I have long detested the past.

Having raised my heart up high
I proclaim to those grieving in tears:
happy are those who bury with a cheerful sigh.

Its passing makes joy more truly felt
and it's changing shape as it evolves.
And joys arrive on a steady conveyor belt.

Things are best when they first appear,
toss those spinster memories away
and grab the day with freedom and cheer.

Shrug your shoulder even if it's old
when uselessly fancy shadows
sneak back to you from the past to unfold.

Those no longer with us never were,
free yourself and move on fast,
to remember is to be a prisoner.

Life is but a minute flitting by.
Kiss each of them goodbye with due haste,
in the present even suffering can satisfy.

The past will never make me its prey.
However wretched the present may be,
I close my eyes and embrace the day.

Endre Ady

LONGING TO BELONG

(*Szeretném ha szeretnének*)

Neither an heir, nor a forebear,
Neither kin, nor someone you know,
I belong to no one, nowhere,
Neither a friend nor a foe.

I'm the highland, like every man,
Arctic, cryptic, without a clan,
A phantom faraway,
A phantom faraway.

But it's a mask I can't maintain,
I must let people see my pain,
Let them see me, if they can,
Let them see just who I am.

My tortured song tells me to yearn
For love that then I'll have to spurn,
Longing always to belong,
Always longing to belong.

Endre Ady

IN THE WASTELAND OF HUNGARY

(*A magyar ugaron*)

I'm wading through a lush landscape:
The old sod bears wild greenery.
I know this weed-worn fallow field,
The Wasteland of my Hungary.

I stoop down to the sacred dirt:
The virgin soil sings of doom.
Hey, you cloud-embracing vines,
Can't any of you ever bloom?

The drunken tendrils twirl as I
Come upon the fallow's sleeping soul,
The fragrance of dead flowers starts
To lovingly unroll.

Then silence. Dragged down by the bramble
I fall asleep beneath the vine,
A gust of laughter swoops down
On these Wasteland Plains of mine.

DUEL WITH THE HOG-HEADED MISTER BIG

(*Harc a Nagyúrral*)

He'll surely kill me, I thought, he'll kill me,
the hog-headed Mister Big, unless I hold
him back. He was grinning at me
and sitting on his gold, whole sacks of gold,
ready to kill me, should I be bold.

I was patting his bristly hog back,
all that ugly fat. He was shimmering.
"Look at me, see who I am," I split
my skull open for him to look and think.
He just laughed after seeing everything.

(Does he see a wild adventurer
of wild desires?) My knees lost their hold.
We were on the shore of bustling life,
the two of us, it was getting dark and cold.
"Your gold, please let me have your gold."

"The next moment could easily kill me,
I haven't got a moment more to waste,
The siren songs of new pleasures are
calling me, new words of toxic taste.
I haven't got a moment more to waste."

"Your heart is protected by fat and bristle,
inside I'm full of pus and guile,
yet my heart is blessed: and also
corroded by life and cruel desire.
Must go. And it's gold the roads require."

"The sea is waiting for my pleasure boat,
and so are pavilions in a parade.
A strange new sun, dabs of exotic balm,
foreign frenzy, many an alien maid,
all waiting for me, for me they were made."

"Life itself still breathes inside me,
all that's new comes galloping my way,
a sacred dance swirls all my dreams.
In you only pangs of deafness sway,
so cut open your golden hump today."

A blue and blind night broke over us,
I was whimpering. The ripples told
the same message over and over again:
We're waiting. Have you got the gold?
That's what the roaring ripples told.

At last, we clashed. The shore trembled,
I fought him hands sunk into fat, I was tough,
tearing him apart. But all in vain.
His gold was jingling. His laugh was rough.
There's no way open, I cannot take off.

A thousand nights have passed since then,
I'm bleeding like a clumsily stuck pig,
distant siren calls come tempting me,
but we're mired in this dueling gig,
I and the hog-headed Mister Big.

Endre Ady

REMEMBERING A SUMMER NIGHT

(*Emlékezés egy nyár-éjszakára*)

A wrathful angel beat the drum
sending alarm from Heaven to Earth,
at least a hundred youths went tight,
at least a hundred stars fell off the sky,
at least a hundred girls gave birth:
a curious,
it was a curious summer night.
Our beehives caught on fire,
our best pony broke a leg,
I dreamed of the dead as if still living,
our faithful dog just passed from sight,
and Mari, our mute maid, quite soon,
broke into a raucous marching tune:
curious,
it was a curious summer night.
Pip-squeaks started strutting bravely,
honest, true men had to lie low,
even picky burglars took a bite:
curious,
it was a curious summer night.
Man was known as a fickle creature,
yet it was funny how things turned
from the past to the living world.
The smiley Moon was full of jeers,
man had never been so slight
as on that very sudden night:
curious,
it was a curious summer night.
With its grinning, scathing sneers
horror let all souls feel its might,
the cryptic fate of their forebears
entered into all of us alive;
Thought, already drunk, took off
for a blood-fueled wedding rite;

that respected servant of Man
turned out to be helpless, paralyzed:
curious,
it was a curious summer night.
I believed then and I was right,
that a neglected God would come back
to life and make me meet my death;
yet look, I am still alive
as someone remade by that night,
still waiting for God to turn up
and still remembering that horrible night
that sank the world and all its might:
curious,
it was a curious night.

Aug 1914

CADAVER ON THE WHEATFIELD
(*Hulla a búzaföldön*)

Left behind on a field covered with snow
In a grave that was never dug and
Where no wormwood or basil will grow.

It seeps in silence into the ground,
The triumphant wheat kernels will drive
Their offspring through it heaven-bound.

Come summer, it'll lie flat as debris,
Like a scarecrow knocked down for fun,
Holding on its chest a golden sea.

Its flattening fate now roars far off,
Again Life, full of hopes and lies,
Flowers from the corpse and above.

1915

THE JÁNOS OF FAIRY TALES

(*A mesebeli János*)

The distant city's in big trouble,
It's time to struggle with the Reaper:
Run, János, run and do the struggle.

If a prince or a noble knight
Left a fancy cape behind,
Run, though rags hang on your hide.

If you really want to meet
The princess of the fairy tales,
It's the Dragon you have to beat.

Nothing but tales and cursed jokes
Have kept things going so far,
A shrug is as good as a hoax.

Nothing about this is new or vague,
You've had plenty of exposure
To seductions of the plague.

You follow orders, that's what you do,
So do it, that's what you're for,
You're tough, it's nothing to you.

If it cripples you at last,
And if you're brave, you'll agonize
over your old sin, the Past.

The great arena wants you today
Even if for your very life
You'll have your own life to pay.

At one time and without regret
You found refuge in a foreign land,
Then run now and don't you mind the sweat.

The princess, János, lives in fairy tales,
But nothing is more alive and stronger
Than them; against them all else fails.

The distant city's in big trouble,
It's time to struggle with the Reaper:
Run, János, run and do the struggle.

1915

MY DOUBTING MAGYAR SOUL
(*Kétkedő, magyar lelkem*)

My army and my people,
All in all, I love you all.

Seeing you pursuing and pursued,
I root for you, foolishly fired up.

It hurts me seeing you like that,
Sad and egged on by Fate.

It hurts me that now I hold my
Sharp throat numbed by a noose.

Hogs are standing in my way
Oinking and forbidding.

My sobering howls shrivel up in
The wasteland of the grand command.

I'd like to gather my own army,
To turn things back the way they were.

I only hope my doubting Magyar soul
Will be proven wrong some day.

September 1915

Endre Ady

THE MUSIC OF AUTUMN

(*Az ősz muzsikája*)

Now again together Silence and Noise,
The Fall has only changed inside us;
Its ancient music and noble joys
Can still be found by a loving heart.

Its tears and sorrows are still the same,
Its songs are just like they used to be,
It can still tell old bedtime tales
But also dig into ancient wounds.

Those brave enough to live are grand;
Their forgetful smiles are precious,
Life-sustaining children and
Their tears are each a dead reborn.

1915

THE NEW HARVEST SONG

(*Új arató ének*)

Crosses settle harvested land,
Crosses in cemeteries,
Crosses on shoulders, in hearts,
Crosses as far as the eye can see,
Only the crucified of the Cross is missed.

Crosses all over the World,
Crosses on steeples and on chests,
Crosses on earthly benevolence,
And the voice from Heaven: "I deserve it;
Why did I go on the cross for these?"

1915

Endre Ady

LEADING THE DEAD BRIGADE

(*A halottak élén, 1917*)

Everyone loses in the Battlefield now,
Clouds of blood are running wild,
Just now I've come upon my loyal troops,
Just now I've come upon my own kind,
Those exiled forever from Life.

Lively, dear, good old boys,
You awakening from the dead,
How I enjoy unsheathing my sword
Before the holy rank for which you bled
And for coming upon you all.

Never had more heroic brothers,
Never like the ones I have now,
The sky-banging shiny helmets are
The midnight moonlight on their brow,
As hey rise from freshly dug graves.

Oh, how long I've been waiting,
I, the orphaned, lonely Cain,
But look, suddenly they joined me,
My troops, my pals, as if never slain,
Never losers of the spirit.

I wonder what they saw back when
Walking on the Battlefield with me,
My pals, brothers assigned to me,
Stripped themselves of their lives,
And look, how they smile with rigid eyes.

True, we all belong to the Life,
And if our souls happened to collide;
It was just life running over in us,
And now, over the graves we abide
One another's multicolored goals.

How lovely this ghostly world is,
To me, it's almost like happiness:
I'm playing the chief commander
In the camp of the truly colorless,
Ordering them all to give Life smile.

Endre Ady

CHRONICLE SONG FROM 1918

(*Krónikás ének 1918-ból*)

Horrors have come to pass and are still on the go,
Nations have been gathering against all nations,
The guilty and the innocent are one in woe,
But man's biggest loss is the loss of faith.

Demented mothers are giving stillbirth,
Our boys play with death instead of rubber balls,
Our bread ovens have all gone cold one by one,
And our fair virgins are walking the streets.

But this wretched mankind is not yet weary,
Foolish and tired but still capable of joy,
These wretched men manage to erase all from
Their memory by doing nothing but kill and kill.

These wretched men do nothing but kill and kill,
And in their feverish dreams they make peace,
But come morning, they go into rage again,
And go on sinning and dying, dwarfed to beasts.

In the fields of death gallows are being built,
On top of them fat crows are sitting in rows,
They've had their fill of cadavers unlike
These wretched men who're not yet done.

Endre Ady

CHRISTMAS
(*Karácsony*)

I.
A bell begins to peal,
a song sends an appeal,
in its notes gratitude prays,
in my lovely little village
at Christmas time
all souls find a place.

Everyone around
kneels to the ground,
praying with pure love,
in my lovely little village
the Messiah
brings happiness from above.

Headed to the church
a long line is in search,
a long line of the young and old,
in my lovely little village
to our God on high
words of thanks are told.

As if today our God
had come down to our sod
and spread his holy grace
in our lovely little village
every heart today
has only love to embrace.

II.
The rough hubbub of the city
sends my soul to roam;
oh, how nice it would be
to celebrate at home,

with a pure heart
-- like in the days of old –
to say our prayers
and thus shed our cares.

How nice it would be
to forget all for a day,
how nice it would be
to be a child at play,
and with true faith of a child's heart
to make peace
with every nation,
and let love be our salvation.

III.
If this lovely old tale
turned into a true belief,
it would mean for this world
happiness and great relief.
These wretched human beings
would become human again,
for our journey this faith
would be a talisman to gain.
This earthly life would no
longer be a Golgotha curse,
one higher power would
permeate the universe.
There would be no other
religion but this little sigh:
love you one another
and worship God on high...
If the old Christmas tale were
to come true, it would bless
this whole world of ours with
lasting and true happiness.

GIVING THANKS
(*Hála adás*)

I hear bright rays of sunshine bong,
Savor your name on my tongue,
Behold your sacred thunder's chord,
My almighty God, my Lord.
Last night confession gripped my soul:
You were present in all I knew,
In the happy way I sniffed around,
In the tenderness my caresses found,
In my sad eyes' sharpened view.
Today I thank you for being there
Where my being was fulfilled,
Where altars tumble and get rebuilt.
Thank you for my bed, so soft and hard,
Thank you for my first infant whine,
Thank you for my mother's broken heart,
For my youth and youthful sins,
For my doubts and faith in hymns,
For the might of love and pain.
Thanks to you I'm in no one's debt
for all the things I was to get.
I hear bright rays of sunshine bong,
Savor your name on my tongue,
Behold your sacred thunder's chord,
My almighty God, my Lord;
So light is my confessing soul,
Thank you for life, love, joy and woe.
Even for death it's you that I owe.

Endre Ady

THE MAGYAR MESSIAHS

(*A magyar messiások*)

Far saltier are our tears,
And more fantastic tortures try us;
A thousand times more messiahs
Are our Magyar, own Messiahs.

A thousand times they have to die and
The cross they bear does not redeem
Their sin of dreaming; yet what else
Is there for them to do but dream?

Endre Ady

THE LAST SHIPS

(*Az utolsó hajók*)

My soul was a free and faithful sea,
I didn't cause its present plight,
that now it's tired, devoid of waves, and dead,
because I was right, always right.

It was open to all flags,
and every lifeboat on my sea
always found a safe haven on shore.
Yet evil winds now write its tragedy.

Two ships are still struggling to sail it
watching and chasing each other's lane
with ripped-up flags of tired fear
and swaggering disdain.

But what am I to fear or disdain,
and for what purpose to go on?
I'll sink the two ships and give
my soul to the Secretive one.

I ask The Secretive One, Fate, God,
and other Nonesuch to compromise
and leave this faithful sea alone;
it yawns with dead and jaded eyes.

Dezső Kosztolányi

HUNGARIAN POETS CRY OUT TO THE POETS OF EUROPE IN 1919

(Magyar költők sikolya Európa költőihez 1919-ben)

We've fallen so deep we can fall no more,
for us there's no depth nor height.
In our mother's tongue we cry out to the world,
what will happen to our hearts and words
when we face the night?

To you, you distant poets, who can rise up
to the heart of God far from here,
sitting on the ground and raking the ashes
of our words, we cry out in tears,
what's to come? What's yet to fear?

Our poetry is already just a cry for help,
unable to reach out through fire and hell,
more like that of a murdered babe
or of a virgin ravished by armed
military personnel.

(*Published on March 16, 1919*)

Dezső Kosztolányi

THE BEGGAR OF TEARS
(*Könnyek koldusa*)

Once I was a holy vessel.
Pain resided in my heart,
and the nice folks
let me play the poet's part.

Now I'm a beggar, a pauper,
because I've lost what I possessed.
And the tears and tears
overflowed the world's every nest.

The world is shaken by the sobs,
everyone weeps and cries in verse,
blind laments,
howling pain into the dark universe.

But the most enormous pain is mine;
here I stand in a flood of woe,
among weepers,
and I have no wound, nor tears to show.

Dezső Kosztolányi

A FLAG

(*Zászló*)

Just a pole and fabric,
yet not a pole and fabric
but a flag.

It never stops speaking,
fluttering,
always feverish,
always high on something,
high above the street,
always about to take off
up into the sky,
always raving
about something,
even when unnoticed and ignored,
like when the city sleeps,
day and night,
already withered
to skin and bone
like a scrawny evangelist,
standing atop a gable,
alone,
wrestling with silence and storms
to no good but with growing grace,
it keeps on flapping,
keeps on speaking out.

You too, my soul, you too –
not just a pole and fabric –
be a flag.

Mihály Babits

THE YOUNG SOLDIER
(*Fiatal katona*)

He barely lived to taste living while
casting a fearless glance around;
the sky and earth returned his smile –
    but he'll have nothing to show:
beauty, health, youthful zesty juice,
learning, knowledge, divine vein,
female eyes saying yes – what's the use
    if that's it, he has to go?

But off he goes without a word,
says a dry-eyed goodbye to his mother
though his soul swims in love immersed:
    he never learned to hate.
He who hated hate in any form
and loved love to reciprocate,
can't have that for which he was born;
    he has to kill and devastate.

He didn't exchange a ring for a ring,
but his heart, his gold for steel;
his treasures surpassed anything
    this world offers you to buy:
his golden heart, his golden grin –
all for us and all for free, and he'll
never even know if we'll lose or win,
    because he'll die if he must die.

(*1916*)

Mihály Babits

EVENING QUESTIONS
(*Esti kérdés*)

When the evening, that gentle covering,
black and smooth and velvety,
is spread out by a giant nanny
to cover the beloved earth so tenderly
and with so much care that every
grass blade can stay standing straight,
no wrinkles will touch one flower
and no butterfly wing will lose its plate
of rainbow colored enamel glaze,
and they will all sleep below this sheet,
in the shade of this velvety veil,
bearing it will be an easy feat:
lose yourself in reverie about the past,
in the sweet torture of memory
of times long past that still can cast
a shifting light patch on and off,
the kind a magic lantern makes you see
and whose remembrance is never cold,
may be a burden but of great price:
your memory-laden head is hard to hold,
except if it on a marble tablet lies:
ambling among so much beauty
questions will though do their duty:
all this beauty and what's the use?
craven questions will make you muse,
what's the silky water, the marble for?
why the evening, its wide-winged cloak?
why the foliage, why the gentle hills?
why the sea waves that no farmer tills?
why the Danaids, a breeze's tender stroke?
why the ditches, why the dykes,
why the sun, that burning rock of heights?
why the memories of times long past?
why the lanterns that do not last?

why the flow of time with no end to gain?
or just look at the humble blade of grass:
why does it grow only to dry and pass?
why does it dry up only to grow again?

HEGESO'S STELE
(Hegeso sírja)

Asleep for two thousand years, my beloved,
dead two thousand years and waiting for me.
Her name is Hegeso. – Marble-colored from
toes to face – a girl of Greek gravity.

Alive though even her breath is silent,
Her breasts too full for the chiton to veil,
What thoughts may swarm under her curls?
She's sitting bent over. Placid. Pail.

Before her stands her servant maid
holding for her a bejeweled jewelry case
and waiting for a selection to be made.

She may be (if my hope is not too late!)
picking out a piece to adorn her face
when I come to her as her promised mate.

DEPARTURE FOR OLD AGE

(*Indulás az öreg korba*)

Bathed in the tick-tock of the clock,
the tiny moments' ripples attack
and sneak me slowly to a distant land
where there'll be no turning back.

They carry me along, but the show
On the shore is so slow, it's a flop.
And yet trees and houses pass me by,
There's no point screaming: "Stop!"

What to wear for the trip? What to pack?
What equipment will I need?
It's like planning an arctic expedition,
to regions where the cold goes deep,

where only green ice, deceitful Northern
Lights and whitish fog banks roam;
that's how I have to plan the journey
that'll never bring me home.

I can see my fate already...
It'll be a cruel and unforgiving trek!
No helicopter or Coast Guard cutter
will ever come to save my neck.

Happy is he who treks the arctic ice,
A venture of hope and doubt for the brave.
My journey has but one possible
And certain outcome: the grave.

Sándor Reményik

THE CHURCH AND THE SCHOOL

(*Templom és iskola*)

Your fight's intended to do no harm,
God will be your witness here,
But there's none amongst you
Who'd refuse to persevere.
God guarantees you the right
To fight for his laws to rule:
Don't give up the house of worship,
Don't give up the church and school!

You respect the law and order
That provides the grounds for peace.
But why shouldn't you hear god's word
In Hungarian, if you so please?
Why shouldn't children hear their parents'
Language as their teachers' tool?
Don't give up the house of worship,
Don't give up the church and school!

As a young lad I used to sprint
Between the schoolyard and the church,
A cool wall for my fevered forehead
Being the object of my search.
Many a time I still return to relive
The springtime of a gentle fool.
Don't give up the house of worship,
Don't give up the church and school!

Even a beggar, a pariah or
A vagabond is given the right
To worship in his native tongue,
To seek his God' help in his plight.
Why's our church the tent of the sky
Over the dirt road's dusty pool?
Don't give up the house of worship,
Don't give up the church and school!

In your tiny whitewashed churches
Now so much power can accrue,
In the tiny whitewashed pews
Even the dead sit down with you.
In the eyes of your grandparents
The command is harsh yet beautiful:
Don't give up the house of worship,
Don't give up the church and school!

1925

THE DESERTER LILY BLOOM

(*Elpártolt liliomszál*)

You lily bloom, you lily bloom,
Why a stranger for your groom?
Why his arm around your waist,
Why forget your ancient race?
Your family and your name
You burned up in your loving flame,
Its glow is seen from faraway,
But what when soon it turns to gray?

You lily bloom, you lily bloom,
Why a stranger for your groom?
Your dad and mom both cried for you,
Crying they let this bond ensue.
You may be very dear to him:
His world is different within.
Your world will melt into his world,
And such union is always cursed.

You lily bloom, you lily bloom,
Why a stranger for your groom?
The seed, the child inside you sprung
Will never learn your lily tongue.
His little soul will wither torn,
It's himself that he will scorn.
Between two fires his mixed blood
Will be shed in frontline mud.

You lily bloom, you lily bloom,
Just keep on bending to your groom.
Loving closeness in your youth
Serves you now as your truth.
In deep sadness we stand around,
Feeling our truth is in the ground,
We cry about the wedding feast,
Inside you our kind has ceased.

1933

Sándor Reményik

ANY WAY YOU CAN

(*Ahogy lehet*)

With patience that makes us grind our teeth,
With lips clamped tightly shut,
With Christ-like effort that wrenches the gut,
Then with spite, ready to spurt,
With a strangled phrase, a swallowed word,
With a hand, open and always free of risk
For only in a pocket can it form a fist,
With an embittered, helpless laugh,
Accepting every legal paragraph,
No longer wondering – and yet wonderstruck
By one thing or another that has betrayed our luck:
My brothers, I say it again, let us bear this life
Whose only fruit is unbearable pain.
Any way we may...

Chanting the psalms of compromise,
We march in an endless chain-gang of prisoners,
We have no weapons, no firearms,
Unarmed is this insurrection of our souls
Although every drop of our blood demands
Peter's sudden move when, in defense of his God,
He abruptly cut off an arresting soldier's ear.
Who are we in truth?
Oh, no, certainly not Humility,
Only the sons of humiliation.
A sagging arch, a swaying bridge between
The proud bridgeheads of generations:

My brothers, we don't live right,
Not a life our fathers would condone.
But let him who could do better than
That throw the first big stone!
Every passing minute is a painful compromise:
Any way we can...
My brother, you stunted hero, the hero of compromise,

Have your words died out or turned into something else?
A spark may still fly out hissing from
The fiery whirlpool that inside you swirls.
The power of flood waters also swells
Inside you in a Niagara-size waterfall.
Be happy if you can fill a glass with clear water
from that roaring stream, that is all.
You get shoved back more and more,
And what's left to you is less and less:
Dig in your heels where you can take a stand
And defend that land beneath your feet, and
The fragment from a fractured phrase,
Along with whatever was allowed to stay:
Any way you may...

Farmlands of Lilliputian size?
A plot of a few square meters that the stone silt
Of a flood could easily destroy.
And yet the sad seed-caster of the Karsts,
The scarecrow of farming work,
Still loves this handful of humus,
He surrounds it with a stone fence,
Even though it could hardly hold his grave.
Oh, the Karst destiny, oh, the Karst burial.

You too, brother, accept your Karst fate,
And defend the Karstland you cultivate,
That handful of humus, too small for your tomb,
That few square meter plot
And those sacred footprints of God
That no assault of the stone flood
Has ever managed to erase.
Defend this plot under your feet,
Your clay pots and the hearth,
The last little morsel of your bread!
But defend it tooth and nail,
With demonic rage and raging joy –
Any way you can...

Any way you may...

Sándor Reményik

THE HUNGARIAN TRICOLOR
(*Három szín*)

The Hungarian tricolor
Has been ripped off our breast
And sent into exile further in,
Inside our heart it found a nest.

As long as our blood is red,
As long as the snow is white,
And the fields in spring grow green,
Our flag remains in our sight:

We'll remember our faith,
To what nation we belong,
Who owns the soil that will take our
Remains with a funeral song,

That our life is like a desert,
A blood-soaked picture is the land,
The aching, cutoff body part
Needs the body for both to stand.

So long as our blood is red,
So long as the snow is white,
And the fields in spring grow green,
Our Hungarian heart will fight:

The Hungarian tricolor may
Be banned and ripped off our breast,
It only migrates further in,
Inside our heart it finds a nest.

For that tricolor will in our heart
Forever burn, bleed and despair;
Those who have ripped it off
Will have to tear it out from there!

1919

Árpád Tóth

YOU DROPPED THE SUN
(*Elejtetted a napot*)

I thought of you this afternoon,
The sun was letting its rays sink
And penetrate my shut eyelids,
Taking on a shade of pink.

The brightness gently lit a fire
On my tired but lax face,
With my eyes shut I was waiting
For the wonted voyage's embrace,

For the silent, unseen ship
To sail off on a magic sea,
For my chaise to start its trip,
In fever waves to rock with me

On its way to the shores of
Fantastically gorgeous lands
Where the splendid home of my
Melancholic daydream stands:

Everything that never really was,
Everything that never will be –
That's how I took off today,
With eyes shut as if by death set free,

Prepared to make believe a life.
Bathing in the care of the sun
Felt as if on my eyelashes
A pink ember shower had begun,

As if cast by a holy light first seen
Before the beginning by the eye
On the bosom of Father God,
Its hunger hard to satisfy.

Then suddenly in a red heat
A thought instructed me to see:
You are very, very far away,
There's nothing, nothing but woe to me.

My eyes popped open with alarm:
On the distant mountaintop
Crimson clouds were gathering
With sorrow that would never stop.

I became at once possessed
By a strange vision with wild force.
Your hands were holding fast the sun
And guiding it today on its course.

That was why it glowed today with
So much brighter, sweeter light,
But this I only realize now
That I'm sitting in the night,

When your tender hands grow tired
And let the sun eventually drop,
That's when in my fading heart
The songs come to a halting stop.

Árpád Tóth

EEVENING SUNRAY WREATH

(*From "Esti sugárkoszorú"*)

Dew spread on the walkway where we strolled,
the weight of shadows plunged across the park,
but sunset weaved the foliage of your hair
into a sunray wreath, so soft and dark...

...For a minute I didn't know if it was you or
a rosebush in bloom standing in for you
with a divine soul from heaven in it
rustling the leaves to give me a clue.

I stood there enthralled in timeless silence,
minutes and millennia passed us by –
Suddenly you took my hand in yours,
and my drooping eyelids went up high;

and I felt an earthly feeling flood back
to my heart in the way blood rushes through
benumbed and tardy arteries in showers of
deep music: it was the love I feel for you!

THE INTERWAR YEARS

Lajos Kassák

A WORKER PORTRAIT
(*Munkásportré*)

God did not create this head in his own image
this head is tortured by the memory of yesterday and the doubt of today
in this head the seeds of revolution are germinating
for this head an executioner has long been laying in ambush
these hands are under the control of a creative spirit
these hands are cursed from right and blessed from the left
these hands can bang down and elevate at the same time
these hands bear the marks of handcuffs
these hands are not clasped in prayer
these hands detest blood
these feet do not slip on an orange peel
these feet connect west with the east
these feet trample over the dragon's seven heads
these feet make their way to regions the head dreams about
this heart is wounded by the tyrant's weapons
this heart renews itself from its own embers
this heart is the twin brother of my heart
this man is like me
under the same sky
we sing
the same song
of sowing
and harvest.

Lajos Kassák

THE ENFORCEMENT OF THE LAW

(*A törvény végrehajtása*)

The good executioner
opens his window.
Peers out over the begonias
he's enormous
like an ox
and infantile.

The good executioner
says his prayers
but the town wakes up
from a frightful dream.

It's proclaimed by trumpets
advertised by posters
the execution is at dawn
at 5 o'clock.

A great day for beggars.
Everyone who can manage it
holds out his hat
begging for loose change.

Dogs start whining.
The prostitutes sneak out
of the police station.

The good executioner gets on his way
and he feels as if he was leading
by hand
his smallest child to Holy Communion.

In the meantime
daybreak comes to earth
and I dive head-first
into the black sea of my ink
where no one can see me.

Lajos Kassák

MAYEM AT NIGHT

(*Az éjszaka zűrzavara*)

The doorbell rang
A horse was standing at the door,
I greeted him with a deep bow,
he saluted with right front leg.

A silver ship rocking me away.
I must've been far from home
on awakening at dawn.

Where have I landed?
I asked in a stupid daze.
What kind of folks live here?
They drained the milk from my glass,
they nailed my bread to the table with iron clamps.

Lajos Kassák

BEFORE MY PAINTINGS

(*Festményeim előtt*)

I'm standing before my pictures
before the pictures
I gave birth to
with great effort
but without sweat
in the hour
of a good day of mine
in broad daylight
in silence
so far from everything
that I'd become indistinguishable
from the real world.
The same fancy tortured me as virgins
the same immobility weighed inside me
as in boulders
and yet the attraction of separation made me fly
toward a color
a form
a line
all the things that
hide my immortality
inside them.

Lajos Kassák

THE END OF THE LEGEND
(*A legenda vége*)

The discarded stone
landed in God's deep lap.
Royal guardsmen
cold-legged whores
worn-out pilgrims
went looking for it in vain.

Using a saxophone
and drums I declare
stop looking for God
he's hiding blind behind the fog
stop looking for the stone
it was a bird with broken wings
it's sleeping in the stomach
of a cat.

I can see
the poor thing.

Attila József

THE SONG OF A GRIEVING HUNGARIAN
(*Bús magyar éneke*)

A song is flying far afield, on raven wings of evening breeze,
a frayed-faced little man is singing, about the things he sees
around him in a silenced land, a Hungary in a daze,
and about summer slipping off, early fall, love and craze.

Toward the heart and eye sockets, his body suffers, pain-possessed;
can he ever rise again, or is he ready for eternal rest?

In the mist of distance his Hungarian song seeks out god,
it can't help but mourn his old home, brothers, his wasted sod.
In Transylvania his rosy mood got mired in cold mud,
In the Northern Highlands, his once-green hope is now a dud.

Toward the heart and eye sockets, his body suffers, pain-possessed;
can he ever rise again, or is he ready for eternal rest?

He's got a zither with strings reaching to the stars' high tiers.
On it he's playing ballads of tearful blood and bloody tears.
Delirious evenings have fled and frozen in the Dolomites,
his bride, a broken lily, unknown she faded from the lights.

Toward the heart and eye sockets, his body suffers, pain-possessed;
can he ever rise again, or is he ready for eternal rest?

He's well past watching for mirages, lets them sail on with their beams,
his eyes are shut and no longer tempted by vain and fickle dreams.
On the graves of pals he spills forget-me-nots out of his hand
and keeps praying: Oh Lord, please, do not forget this land!

Toward the heart and eye sockets, his body suffers, pain-possessed;
but if it helped his land, he'd live forever and never rest.

1923

Attila József

WITH A PURE HEART

(*Tiszta szívvel*)

Fatherless and motherless,
godless and countryless,
I'm without a crib or coffin,
without a lover to possess.

For the third day I have gone
without a meal of any kind.
My twenty years are worth a soup,
it's a buyer I must find.

If no one else will purchase them,
I don't care if the devil will.
With a pure heart I will rob,
if I'm paid, I'll even kill.

So what if I get caught and hanged,
buried under hallowed ground;
over my great, gorgeous heart
deadly grasses will abound.

1925

Attila József

MY MOTHER
(Anyám)

She held a mug between her hands
on a slow Sunday evening,
giving a silent smile she sat
for a while in the dimming light –

She'd brought home the scrappy leftovers
from a fancy family's supper table,
we went to sleep and I could see
them eating from a whole big pot –

My mother was tiny, gone before her time,
because laundresses go fast,
their legs shake from lugging wet clothes,
get headaches from the coal fumes in the iron –

They have piles of laundry for the mountains!
the steam from the wash kettle for
nerve-soothing spectacle of playful clouds,
and the attic with the clothes lines for fresh air–

I see her pause with the iron in her grip.
Her fragile physique was fractured by big
business, she kept getting leaner –
think about it, my fellow working stiffs –

She got bent doing other people's laundry
before I realized she was a young woman;
in her dreams she had a clean apron on,
and the mailman said good morning to her –

Attila József

MAMA

(Mama)

Thoughts of Mama have been on my
mind for the most part of this week.
She had a basket of wet laundry
swaying from her arms with a squeak.

Being a forthright man, I threw
a tantrum, screaming at her I said:
Hand the heaping wash to someone else
and take me around with you instead!

She just kept on walking to the clothesline,
she didn't scold me or stop to stare,
the soggy pieces were soon flying
and shining swirls up in the air.

I'd stop whining, but now it's too late,
though her greatness hits me in the eye –
her gray hair floating high above, she pours
blue bleach in the washtub of the sky.

1932

Attila József

I'LL BE A GARDENER
(Kertész leszek)

I'll be a gardener of trees,
with the rising sun I'll rise
and see to it that none of my
pregnant flowers ever dies.

Pregnant loving flowers will
flock around me in a sea,
and I don't care their kiss can sting
if they're flowers true to me.

I'll drink milk and smoke a pipe,
my good name I will staunchly guard,
no harm can come to me if I
plant myself too in the yard.

There's a great need for this work
in the east and in the west –
when this world dies it will need
flowers on its grave to rest.

IF YOU DON'T...

(Ha nem szorítasz...)

If you don't press me to your bosom
Like the most precious thing you own,
While you're lost in dreams I get
Dismantled by burglars, bone by bone,
And you collapse on the sofa crying:
What a lonely fool you are, I'll moan.

If you don't assure me every minute
You depend on me for a happy mood,
If you can chat up a storm with the gaunt
Shadow about the pain of solitude.
Your love will have not a thread left,
It'll be frazzled, it'll never be renewed.

If you're not clutching me, I'm whacked
By trees, the ocean waves, the sky.
My love for you is like a child's,
Just as cruel and on the sly:
I board up the hall where you
Bathe me in light:--and I die.

Attila József

THE POOR ARE THE POOREST

(*Aki szegény, az a legszegényebb*)

If God were a scribe and kept
Plying his pen all he could do,
He couldn't write a list of all
The sufferings the poor go through.

Poor folks are the poorest of all,
They add their shivers to winter freeze,
Their spare warmth to summer heat,
Their blues to lazy desert breeze.

On weekdays they stay on the job,
Cares shadow their Saturday night,
Sunday may cheer them but so soon
Monday dawn asserts its might.

And yet inside they keep tender doves,
Star-feathered, fair, singing birds,
Hatching griffins though, they'll give
The eagle folks their just deserts.

Attila József

MY HOMELAND

(*Hazám*)

The rich live in fear of the poor,
and the poor in fear of the rich.
Cunning fear is ruling us,
not only hope's fickle twitch.

Those munching on the peasant's bread
would not give him his fair share,
the migrant worker dries like straw,
but he still demands what's fair.

From a distance of a thousand years
the son of the people appears
with a bundle on his back,

looking for a doorman's job.
Yet instead, he should take a rod
and give his father's grave a whack.

Attila József

PROFIT

(*Haszon*)

Knead bread dough by gaslight at dawn;
or fire hole-ridden red bricks;
let a hoe give you calluses;
lift your skirt when turning tricks;
board up mineshafts on your back;
lug huge pails without a rest;
drop out of school or learn a trade –
you stand before the profit's desk.

Rinse silk shirts in chemicals;
dig up onions on the crawl;
wear a gold-trimmed doorman's hat;
tailor pants for short and tall;
keep it up when you start to lag!
What if you get sacked by the boss?
Will you beg? Or steal? Watch the law –
you stand here, and profit sits across.

Fabricate lovelorn poetry;
hang smoked hams on heavy hooks;
pick wildflowers for herbal tea;
keep accounts and cook the books;
slaughter goats that bray at you;
sleep at the Ritz or on forest moss –
by the time your pay is due,
you stand here, and profit sits across.

Attila, you know the word;
you don't live on salmon sauce –
whether idle or at work,
you stand here, and profit sits across.

IT'S NOT ME YELLING
(*Nem én kiáltok*)

It's not me yelling, the earth turned wild,
you'd better watch out, Satan has gone berserk.
Lie low at the clean bottom of springs,
flatten yourself into a plate glass pane,
hide behind the gleam of diamonds,
under rocks, among bugs,
conceal yourself in freshly baked bread,
you wretched indigent.
Seep into the ground with fresh showers –
it's no use washing your face within,
you must do it in someone else.
Be a tiny cutting edge on a blade of grass
and you'll be bigger than the axle of the world.
O, machines, songbirds, tree leaves, stars!
Our barren mother is begging for a child.
My friend, my beloved friend,
whether horrible or magnificent,
it's not me yelling, the earth turned wild.

Attila József

CHRISTMAS
(Karácsony)

It must be at least twenty below,
winds and people are singing,
leaves are dead, but a man was born.
Farmlands are seriously pondering
our warm faith in sowing seeds,
with unwavering love, the streets are guiding
all the hearts that rush about.
Only sad affection sees the benefit of
having cut no openings for windows;
we warm up one another inside without firewood.
But where will begonias go?
The sky sings with us in tune above,
and behind every shivering forehead
the newborn builds a fire with budding twigs.

Attila József

FOR MY BIRTHDAY

(*Születésnapomra*)

Today I'm turning thirty two,
for a gift this verse will do,
gimcrack
knickknack:

in a nook of this café
it's the surprise of the day
from me
to me.

Thirty-two years have slipped away,
never earned me a monthly pay.
How grand,
my Land!

I tried wielding chalk rather then
a poet's unwieldy fountain pen,
a sad
old lad.

But no good teach became of me,
dismissed by a university
nitwit
bigwig.

His admonition still hits home
for my "With a Pure Heart" poem,
tried hard
to guard

the land against the likes of me.
With my spirit eyes I still can see
his flame
and name:

"As long as I live you'll never fare
as a high school teacher anywhere,"
            he blows
            and glows.

If it warms Professor Horger's heart
this poet's given up grammar art,
            his joy
            poor toy –

a high school is not my end,
it's the whole nation I intend
            to reach
            and teach!

1937

GOD

(*Isten*)

I've seen your mountains, my Lord,
and they made me feel so small.
I'd like to be big like you, my Lord,
so that I could sit on your threshold.
I'd place my heart there,
but how would you like that puny little thing?
Its stutter would get lost in
the pulse of your enormous mountains,
and sadness sleeps under my bed.
Why can't I teach my heart to sing?
Like the mountains and their grasses
whose heart has green fires going
that can guide all the tired insects home in the evening
and you stand there with open arms,
bubbling with serenity at the end of the road –
I should not disturb your work, oh Lord,
but let me look beyond the flowers of the field.

Attila József

NO ONE WILL HELP ME UP

(*Nem emel fel*)

No one will help me up again,
I'm in the mud, deeply mired.
Adopt me for a son, my God,
don't let me stay an orphan child.

Put me back together with your
creative hands for the dual job
of denying and confessing you,
please help me do both, my God.

You know what a brat I am –
don't return my denying you;
don't make my soul blind, but let
it catch a glimpse of heaven too.

Already indifferent to pain,
I've taken on myself your cares,
but now I ask you to watch
over my shadow-land prayers.

Urge my loved ones to be more
forbearing to me and nice.
Please review my case on file
before my final sacrifice.

Jenő Dsida

HYMN TO SNOWFALLS TO COME

(Jövendő havak himnusza)

Hail you wholesome, pure white snow,
sparkling with unlimited whiteness,
consoling us with daybreak glow
on long nights of frozen darkness –
Hail you blessed, pure white snow!

Hail you silence purified,
in which angelic flakes are afloat
and throbbing accolades abide
like snow-clad branches toward the sky –
Hail you, silence pacified!

Hail inscrutable mystery,
the landscape of our future yet untouched
by skates where we
go sledding on our far-reaching dreams –
Hail you, virgin mystery!

Hail you, coming Messenger,
you tell our muddy, desolate little world,
covering it with fuzzy ermine fur:
"Go to sleep you roof! And you tower too!
Hail you, mysterious Messenger!"

Jenő Dsida

NOCTURNAL VISIT
(Éji látogatás)

Can't avoid looking into the prison cell
of the soul at night when the dark is huge
and the guards are asleep.

Hands entangled in a fight
the night of the cell echoes:
– Six elbows to the left,
six elbows to the right –
I'm crazed with fright!
Crazed with fright! –

Outside a wind blindly crows.

1925

Jenő Dsida

TWILIGHT
(Alkony)

Cool September. Twilight.
The grayish lake
is one eye of a ghost.
The other one is my shut soul.

Roaring trees in convulsions:
punctured, horrible spiders,
they snap at us, trying to
recapture their prey.

Scattered autumn leaves,
we're fleeing, on the run,
ahead the windows of a distant
mansion light up signaling to us.

Jenő Dsida

NOTHING'S DREAM
(*A Semmi álma*)

Nothing has dozed off
and dreamed of becoming Something,
none other than me!

And dreamed of a Aim gleaming
at me from faraway,
an unknown Aim
toward which I make my way…

And there are travelers coming
And asking: where from?
And I answer: I don't know!
And they ask me: where to?
And I answer: I don't know!

Dusk is sneaking up on us,
The green fields melt into purple,
Blue mountains into gray,
And, with head hanging low
I keep going, making my way!…

Nothing has the craziest dreams!

1924

Jenő Dsida

SHADOW ON THE WALL

(*Árnyék a falon*)

Reckless and furiously dark,
that shadow cursed me with a sign,
on a moonlit wall sharply drawn,
that shadow of a shadow of mine!

A hard-hearted, defiant fighter,
an ancestral haughty knight
who gets up from his grave to visit
and stare me in the eye every night.

I fear someday he'll step on me and stomp
me into the ground like a frog...
I stare back at him with glassy eyes,
a shadow of his shadow from the fog.

At least he knows: he's very sad,
at least he knows: he's as dark as night,
at least he knows, his sword at the ready,
he's always there, prepared to fight.

But what do I know? Nothing, nothing,
I don't know who I am or what to believe,
am I whooping it up with a gypsy band
or weeping in mortal grief?

I keep looking at the moonlit shadow,
in a cold shiver and hot fever fed
by ancient myths, superstitious fear,
and I can't help it but bow my head.

1924

Jenő Dsida

THE LAST *OUR FATHER*
(*Az utolsó Miatyánk*)

Miniscule little pill.
Time to turn out the light.
Our Father who art in Heaven!
Another scream in the night.

To fall asleep, to fall asleep,
serenity, silence and peace.
Hallowed be thy name!
Is there an end to these?

Sighs the visitor in dark,
Lucky are those who die.
May thy kingdom come!
I'm beginning to feel high.

Stars begin to blink,
Beckoning with glee.
Let Thy will be done!
It's all the same to me.

CYANIDE, HANDGUN
(*Méreg, revolver*)

Get yourself cyanide, a handgun or under a train!
Slit your croaking throat,
you damned fool!
—Take a look: someone's stealing
your eyes from under your brow,
hitching his carriage to your desires
instead of horses, resoling his shoes
with your warm heart and building
a golden palace for himself out of your misery –
Take a look: hundreds of thousands,
millions are shriveling up into graves,
miserable beasts, your brothers
who at one time had
the faith and the will
just like you—Oh,
open your unhappy eyes,
you miserable,
newly arrived young man,
you gullible, you crazy fool,
and go home,
stand in front of the mirror,
place the straight razor on your neck—
—then run amok
on the evening boulevard
and toss the howling bomb
of your severed head into the window of
the first happy man!

1926

Lőrinc Szabó

WILD WEST EUROPE
(*Wild West Európa*)

In big cities, in the asphalt
prairies of money,
helpless herds are running around
all day for nourishing
grass. But meat is
good enough for some,
meat and the gold hidden in it:
open season on prey,
heroes are zooming around on motorcycles,
newly invented weapons are rattling
without a sound, new victories are entered
into ledgers by offices—
and in the evening
in the festive stables of sex
the smartest fratricidal maniacs are
saluted in unison
by two hundred
naked female thighs.

1926

HOUSES, PALACES, BALDHEADED THIEVES
(*Házak, paloták, kopasz bűnösök*)

Stone houses, streets, lights of the night,
I come from fields of divine delights.
Houses, palaces, baldheaded thieves:
what am I doing in the midst of these?
Houses, money, business, men and dames;
death floats over their ruined remains.
Death can build things and turn them to ash,
rotting world, a giant heap of trash!
Houses, palaces, baldheaded thieves:
what am I doing in the midst of these?
What am I... into a horrible prison hurled!
What am I doing in this soulless world?

1926

Lőrinc Szabó

THERE'S NO MONEY AND WE MUST EAT

(*Nincs pénz és enni kell*)

There's no money, and you tell me to forget it,
There's no money and we're having a fine spring, --
There's no money, but you've never
Embraced the man outside of time into your misery,
You've never seen a single simple example of
The timeless law governing the dispossessed
And the justification of evil-doers:
There's no money even though it's a question
Of naked existence!—How am I to put springs
into my steps when I rush to greet tomorrow
when
there's no money, and there are folks
waiting for me at home, my loved ones
and innocents, hungry for
bread—oh, how can I laugh
when there's no money,
and life can be purchased for money, and
there's no money,
and we must eat,
and someone inside me keeps
whispering and roaring that
all is a craven lie, the suit
I wear tells a lie, so do my shoes
And the moment that sometimes
Seduces me to enter a cinema, the sin palace
Of Sound and Color—oh,
How can I bother with
Beauty, the heavenly beloved
of the soul when
there's no money, and there are
folks waiting for me at home,
loved ones, innocent and hungry
for bread—why should I proclaim
life is worth living

even if you're poor, and
there's no money,
and you must eat, and in me too
the curse of bread has broken
all will to live—how could I
be happy when wherever I look I
only see
the Needs of the Body hovering
over the black republic
of poverty, and the eternal
tyrant of Physical Existence and
Organized Money
Who stands with the disembodied
Horror of his foot on our throat
Without though squashing us like a worm
And who, flashing
Distant light signals into our
Invisible night prevents its
Partner in us from falling asleep,
Its naïve little partner, hope!

1926

Lőrinc Szabó

EXPLOSIONS

(*Robbanások*)

It all became a metaphor when faith
and feverish desire conquered sin and cures,
you opened up, and my fountain-driven heart
began to gush from my mouth into yours

in strict silence, like a lover who takes on death
in struggle for air, yet drunk on blood and fire,
in search of your gate he suddenly sensed he was
pushing his way freely inside your empire

toward your heart, through caves of flesh,
through silkiness, signaled early by your lips,
the maddening silk walls of a silky kiss:

our thoughts crying out at each other hurled –
when explosions, mute and yet gargantuan,
were shaking, agitating inside us the world.

1950

Lőrinc Szabó

LOUNGING AMONG FLOWERS
(*Virágok közt hevertünk*)

We were lounging among flowers... Not only
you face, but your whole body radiated
its inner light and your tender goodness
m—curvaceous stream—that flooded the whole
evening field, making every flower and blade of
grass lean toward you: toward the Sun.
At first we wordlessly marveled
at the passionate ruddiness of the clouds
flying over god's forehead, then – when
the singing residents of the foliage
have quieted down—bending over
your breasts I felt happy terror rise over
my heart, the fluttering of dusk was
crowning your head:
Earth's blood was flowing from your arm into mine
and voluptuous Flora was kissing me in your kisses.

1922

Lőrinc Szabó

SINCE YOU'RE NOWHERE

(*Mert sehol se vagy*)

Since you're nowhere, I seek you everywhere,
the sun, the fields; a cloud can be your dress,
the world keeps showing you, continues to possess
your essence, even in the way my stare
predictably fails to capture you;
the play of light and shadow, cricket noise
can reproduce the tinkling of your voice,
imagination can always find a clue:
I see you and I don't, your dear name
in my heart always echoes yours,
yet every moment robs me of my claim:
I open myself to the stars and prick my ears,
but while chasing you, this predator is lured
into your grave; into himself he disappears.

1950

Lőrinc Szabó

YOU'RE EVERYWHERE
(*Mindenütt ott vagy*)

You're there, every place I used to know
and love you one or another day,
it's with you that lakes and summits sway
calling me, it's you that rain and snow,
day and night, town and village tell
about in roads and the whistle of the train,
they have the first quaking passion to contain,
plus the twenty five springs of madness spell.
You're there, every place, in a flood of flowers
covering my life, fresh happiness that devours
my refreshing youth and pleasure-filled hours;
everything every place displays your face
for me always with a painfully strangled cry:
I can't find an Every Place any place.

1950

NOTHING ELSE

(*Egyéb nem*)

Since there's no part of her left
I love all that she used to own
Around her, the pillow for her rest,
The bracelet, orphaned objects left alone,
The key that used to lead me to her,
Distant forests, cities, the travel dust
We stirred up together, the smile that
Ran up from her heart to her eyes in a gust
When sitting for a portrait:—no substitute
But the whole world is filled with them,
And it's only now they make me astute:
The sky and earth and all else are a lane
To her: I have to love my thoughts of her
For no other parts of her remain

1950

WARS OF DISTOPIAS

Miklós Radnóti

NO WAY OF KNOWING...
(*Nem tudhatom...*)

I have no way of knowing what this land means to others,
but to me this little country, embraced by flames, is
native soil, the world of my fast-receding childhood.
I grew up from it like a fragile branch out of a tree trunk,
and I hope my remains will some day sink back into it.
I am at home. And if one or another bush kneels at my feet,
I know its name and what kind of flower it bears,
I know where they're headed, who are those marching
on the road, and I know what the reddening pain
gushing out of cottage walls can mean on a summer eve.
To those flying over it, this land is just a map that gives
the pilots no idea where the poet Mihály Vörösmarty lived;
to them this map hides factories and wild barracks, what else?
but to me it has crickets, oxen, steeples, peaceful farms;
those looking through binoculars see factories and fields,
while I also see workers worried about the fruits of their labor,
forests and orchards filled with birds, vineyards and graves,
and among the graves a old granny softly whimpering;
and what looks like target for bombs from above, the workshops
and the railroad tracks, also have a grade-crossing guard
signaling to the train with a red flag and a bunch of kids around,
and there's a dog rolling in the dust of the factory yard;
and there's the park, filled with the footprints of old loves,
the taste of kisses in my mouth, now honey, now rhubarb;
and on the way to school, stepping up to the sidewalk
I used to step on a particular curbstone for good luck,
and look, there's the stone, except you can't see it from above,
there's no instrument that would detect and show all that.

Yes, we know we are a guilty nation just like the others,
we know what sins we've committed, where and how,
but there are workers living here and poets, too, unstained by sin,
and nursing babies with developing minds lit up by reason,
they guard it by hiding it in deep dark cellars until

the finger of peace scrawls a sign on our land once again;
they will answer our strangled words with words of their own.

You guardian cloud of the night, drop your great wing over us.

January, 1944

Miklós Radnóti

THE FUGITIVE
(A bujdosó)

From the window I spy a hill,
but it can't look into my lair;
from my pen poems spill,
though it's all up in air;
I see it, but cannot see why
this old-fashioned boon;
like before, the moon scales the sky,
and cherry trees begin to bloom.

May 9, 1944

Miklós Radnóti

RAZGLEDNICAS
(*Razglednicák*)

1. From Bulgaria wild cannon fires thunder
and thud on the hillcrest before going under;
there's a traffic jam of people, beasts, carts and thought,
neighing the road rears, the sky runs with mane distraught.
You're a landmark inside me in this hullabaloo,
deep in my soul you shine, forever still and true,
like a silent angel, amazed at the tragedy,
or like a bee boring into the bark of a dying tree.

In the mountains, August 30, 1944

2. Six miles from here houses and haystacks are
aflame, and at this farm,
sitting at the field's edge, peasants light up
their pipes in mute alarm.
Wading in, the little shepherdess
makes ripples of the puddle's peace
as the sheep lean over the water
slurping up a cloud's fleece.

Cservenka, October 6, 1944

3. Blood is what the oxen salivate,
blood is what most people urinate,
the work platoon stands still in wild clumps of stink.
Death above us drives its dreadful wind.

Mohács, October 24, 1944

4. I hit the ground beside his corpse; it flipped,
already as stiff as a string about to break.
Shot in the back of the head. "You'll be next",
I told myself. "Just lie still, without a quake.
It's death that blooms from patience here."
"Der spingt noch auf," someone barked above.
A crust of blood and mud dried up on my ear.

Szentkirályszabadja, October 31, 1944

Sándor Márai

EPILOGUE

(*Utóirat*)

A magician who believes and believes not,
Abandoned by his friends and even God,
Whispering obsessively in a loud cry,
Flings his wild magic words at the sky.
That's how I want to give my secret away,
The word is prone to fly, the flesh to decay.
But something harder than words or matter
Has touched my soul, and now wounds batter
My body like a leper's, pain projects the Sign,
Marked by this world, I'm waiting for my time.
I've seen the secret, can't just mutely run,
The smoke of sin has eclipsed the sun.
I've seen the other shore, entranced by
The dark glow, where the lightning fire
Rises and sets, Satan's nightmare briar.
The world is far away; here the horrible toys
Of war are howling in a leaden voice.
Sin's hot embers are singeing everything:
Christians, Jews, and Europeans who think.
Encrusted with blood is every trusted door,
Murdered are those worthy of trust,
Debased is all that was worth living for.
Your bed is a coffin, a crypt that reeks.
Traded are believers and beliefs.
Apocalypse has opened wide its gates,
The sky's blood is crying out to testify.
The one who kissed you, kissed you goodbye.
The one you hug tonight will not see the sun.
You're held and sold by the same loved one.
I'm sitting at land's end in Babylon,
Listening to death incessantly rattle on.
The roar of water, earth and sky is heard,
Learn to grieve when you inter the world,
Cry hard when you cry for all who died,
Your pen has only epitaphs to inscribe.

Dec 1944, Budapest

Sándor Márai

ANGEL FROM HEAVEN,

you must make your way
To smoldering Budapest without delay.
To a wintery city you must intrude
Where Russian tanks roar and bells are mute.
Where Christmas lights are now a luxury,
No golden fruits are hanging from the tree,
There's nothing but hunger and shivering cold.
Tell them all and the way it must be told.
Your voice in the night must not relent:
Bring them news of the wondrous event.

Flap your wings with all deliberate speed,
Waiting for you are some folks in need.
Don't talk about the world out there,
About warm houses lit by candle flare
Where dinner tables are now being set,
The priest is soothing, tells you not to fret,
Wrapping paper rustles with the gift,
Words of wisdom hand out moral lift.
Sparklers lend the trees light and scent;
Angel, tell them of the wondrous event.

Announce the world's great new mystery:
A long-suffering people's Christmas tree
Was set on fire in the Silent Night—
So many now cross themselves at the sight.
The peoples of every crowded continent
Just keep staring; it's so hard to comprehend.
Some shake their heads as they turn away,
Some just pray, yet some back off in dismay;
It's not candy hanging from the tree
But the Christ of all peoples, Hungary.

There are so many who played a part:
The Soldier who stabbed Him in the heart;
The Pharisee who sold Him out in the end,
The one three times gainsaid being a friend;

One kept washing hands clean in a bowl
Thirty pieces of silver was one's goal
And heaping curses another would thresh,
Drinking innocent blood and eating flesh–
The multitudes can only stand and stare
But to speak to the victim they don't dare.

He speaks no more, nor does he sue,
A Christ on the cross just looks at you.
How peculiar is this Christmas tree,
Brought by an Angel or some devilry—
Those busy throwing dice for the cloak
Know not what they do, they're just plain folk,
Although they sniff and snort and suspect
The great secret of the night of unrest,
This Christmas is filled with much unease:
The Hungarian people hang from the trees.

The world keeps talking of the mystery,
Priests sermonize about the bravery;
Wrapped in caution statesmen sympathize,
The Pope sends his blessings and his sighs.
People regardless of beliefs or class
Question why this ever had to pass.
Why didn't they perish like it was meant?
Why didn't they just wait for the end?
Why was the sky rent with a great puff
When a people said: "That's enough."

The peoples of the world still can't understand:
What tsunami has hit this fateful land?
What shook the whole world order up like hell?
One people cried out. And then silence fell.
But some still ask: What was it about?
Over flesh and bones, who wields the clout?
They keep asking with hesitant intent,
More and more, for they can't comprehend—
They who got it with their family tree—
What's the big deal about this Liberty?...

Angel, your news from Heaven must be spread,
Blood breeds new life every time it's shed.
They meet often in pastures or in the wild
—the donkey, the shepherd, and the child—
Beside the manger lying down in straws,
When Life begets the new life without a pause,
The Wonder is still there for them to guard,
With their panting breath they watch it hard,
Dawn is breaking, but the Star is not yet spent,
Go tell them—
you, angel from Heaven sent.

(*"Mennyből az angyal"*) *New York, 1956*

Gyula Illyés

TYRANNY IN ONE SENTENCE

(*Egy mondat a zsarnokságról*)

Where there is tyranny
it's tyranny that rules
not only from the gun barrels,
not only in the deep dark pools

of prison cells and
interrogation rooms,
in the midnight wake-up calls,
it's tyranny that looms

not only in the smoke and mirror
of the prosecutor's tale,
in the pliant guilty pleas,
in the word tapped through the jail,

not only in the judge's jaded
verdict: guilty as charged!
it's tyranny that rules in
the military orders barked,

in the "attention!", in the "fire!",
in the drum's deadly roll
as the corpse is dragged
into a common hole,

not only in the news
whispered through half-open doors
by lips that fearful twitching
never long ignores,

in the finger raised against the lips
silently saying shush,
it's tyranny that rules
not only in the grill-work bush
of facial wrinkles woven

like a prison wall
for a wordless cry of woe,
in the waterfall

of silent tears that flow
from a mute eye socket
missing its eyeball,

feeding them on its smile
it's tyranny that rules
the standing ovations
in frenzied schools;

where there is tyranny
it's tyranny that rules
not only in the clapping hands
as its programmed tools,

in the trumpet, the concert hall,
lilting lies in loud streams
sung by loyal sculptured stones
in galleries, in the color schemes

of all the paintings and already
in the artist's brush;
not only in the midnight car
sliding along without a hush,

in the way it halts
under gateway vaults;

where there is tyranny
its omnipresence is so wide
as your old god never
managed to abide;

it's tyranny that rules
in the daycare centers,
into the father's advice and
the mother's smile it enters,

it palls your child's every word
a stranger may have overheard;

not only in the barbed-wire fence;
in the weighty rows of books
whose slogans rip your soul more surely
than the barbed-wire hooks;

it even rules in the tiny
good-by kiss of the spouse
asking when will you be home,
dear, safe in the house;

in the tone of oft-repeated
hurriedly said how-are-you,
in the suddenly much softer
handshake there may be a clue,

in the way your lover's face
suddenly just freezes up,
it's there with you two on your date,
in the park, the coffee cup,

not only in the questioning
but in the confession's whine,
even in love's sweetest words
like an insect in your wine,

for even in your dreams
you cannot be alone,
it lies in the nuptial bed and
in the first sweet longing moan,

for you can only love what
tyranny once possessed;
it's the tyrant, not your love,
pressed against your chest,

it fogs the bowls and glasses,
coats the nostrils and dry tongues,
it's the draft of darkness
racing through the lungs,

with sunshine through the open window
it sends the stench of a dead dog,
invades the house like a gas leak's
unseen but deadly smog,

talking to yourself you answer,
it's up to the tyranny to ask,
even in your fantasy
finding freedom is a task,

the Milky Way becomes a vast
no-man's land with search-lights scanned,
the stars are peepholes and behind them
millions of jailers stand,

or the teaming night sky is but
one enormous labor camp;
it's tyranny that speaks in public,
from every church bell and street lamp,

but also from the priest in shrift,
or from his holy homily;
the Party Congress or torture rack,
all stage a show for you to see;

you may try blinking but it's still
the same thing looking back at you
and sticks to you like memory,
like a drawn-out flu;

clicking train wheels tell your story,
locked up, locked up, all they say;
this is what you breathe in on
a mountain top or ocean bay;

the smallest noise becomes
a zigzag lightning bolt,
a flash of light ignites a
missing heartbeat's jolt;

even resting you still feel it,
in the shackling boredom's cry,
in a lashing shower storm,
with bars that reach up to the sky,

in the cell-wall whiteness of
the paralyzing snowfall fog;
it's tyranny looking at you
through the eyes of your dog,

because it's there in every goal,
in tomorrow's and the next,
in every move, in every thought,
every gesture and your rest;

like water its own riverbed,
you follow it and dig it out;
want to sneak a glance beyond?
it's tyranny the mirrors tout,

there's no escaping from its eyes,
you're the prisoner and the guard;
it seeps into your cigarette
and the fabric of your garb

and eats its way into
the marrow of your bone;
crave ideals? it's only
ideology you may own,

crave a look? only what it
conjures up is what you see,
a single match stick's flame can
put you in a forest-fire sea,

you didn't stamp it out when
you dropped the match in the loam;
but tyranny watches out for you
from posters at work and at home;

you cannot taste what life is like,
what bread and meat are for,
what it's like to long and love with
arms stretched open any more,

thus the slave prepares his shackles,
on himself he locks the gate;
it's tyranny your soup spoon feeds,
it's for tyranny you procreate,

where there is tyranny
human links make up the chains;
it's from you folks that it reeks,
for tyranny is in your veins;

like moles we stumble in the sun,
blindness fetters our feet,
we perspire in the pantry
as if in Sahara's heat;

where it's tyranny that rules
nothing matters, nothing counts,
you chant its praises faithfully
like the water in the founts,

it's tyranny that stands there
waiting by your grave,
telling you just who you were;
your ashes, too, its slave.

1950-1951

[First published in 1956 during the Uprising as dictated by the poet from memory; that is why the incomplete stanzas which were left intact when the ban on was lifted in the 80's and the poem was accessible to the reading public.]

György Faludy

FAREWELL TO RECSK
(*Búcsú Recsktől*)

We had no pen, no books; to our
depth no news or mail were ever sunk,
we had to make do with a mess kit
and one half of a wooden bunk,
we lived with stoolies and slave drivers,
they beat us and kicked us till half gone
from starvation and the shivers
with the lime pit looking on,
seven days a week we worked
and without a hope we went to bed, --
our eyes met in silence saying:
you too are among the living dead.
And yet – what was it in most of us
that somehow sustained the soul?
Back then I only sensed it but now I know
the secret of that horrible hell hole.
....

I learned to live
extra- and introverted in one,
sensitive and insensitive;
I learned my multi-parted body
and all its components conspired
in great secrecy in order
to save me before I expired, --
me, I say, because I also learned
as long as I'm alive my fate
belongs to two of us; my body
has a soul, too, for a mate,
although every inch of me is
a brother, a comrade-in-arms, a friend,
I am not a sum of them, at
the skin my being doesn't end.

1955

György Faludy

LOVE SONNET (S. 21)

(*Hol válik el, S.21*)

Your flesh and soul play hide and seek,
I can't decide just which is which:
your knees as mystic idols peek
at toenails with a fetish twitch.

Celestial tunes serenely ring
when your shoes tap on the stairs,
our heavenly love is quickening
the ringlets of your pubic hairs.

And what else? You incarcerate
my flesh while opening a gate
to new views for my spirit part.

With every breath I say: I love
you, though a leopard and a dove
destroy you daily in my heart.

(*Malta, 1966*)

WAITING FOR THE NEXT

Sándor Weöres

GOLDEN CORD

(*Aranyzsinór*)

What I need is a thought,
maybe like a golden cord,
to cut the coming night in half
and to have it safely moored.

Resting in an easy chair
it could survey the night
and its waves of shades with
a new but millennial sight.

What I need is a thought
that rises out of ancient times
and can linger here with us
making ever newer signs.

SUNKEN SIGNS

(*Elsüllyedt jelek*)

Wind erases my tracks.
Mud erases my tracks.
There was a battle in this town,
everything's about to drown,
new tracks erase my tracks.

You, image of god,
do you really want another failure,
what else from an impossible sod?
What else but guard my tracks.

THE RIDER OF THE PLAZA

(*A tér lovasa*)

You are the rider of the plaza,
people flock to you to be roused
carrying sheaves of wheat.
You're the focal point of love,
you are, when you are, man,
and nothing else any more.
You're the question and
you're the false answer.

We all love you, and yet
when you are,
you're not to be expected,
not to be stolen,
next to nothing.

In your tracks
the barking hounds of fright
not to be
silenced
by anything.

Sándor Weöres

LIGHTS GONE OUT
(*Kialudt fények*)

Streetlamps used to give the park
a gentle sunrise glow, but now
oblivion casts a shadow over it.

Unattended silent sorrow
seeks to snake around
anyone passing through,
but no one ever comes.

Fallen branches fill a cart
whose memory still roams here,
gaping at the great sorrow.

Sándor Weöres

AFTER CREATION

(*A teremtés után*)

The first day in hell
after creation is still
bright and clear.

Someone's banging away
over the meadow,
the whole area quakes,
someone's waiting for
the hopelessly-lost.

Someone can see,
is it me?
Someone can touch,
is that me?

There's someone now beyond reach
in the past
who can no longer recognize things
once seen and touched
on a sliver of fog.

Sándor Weöres

THE WORLD OF ENNUI

(*Az unalmas világ*)

I

Through a million flies
A ray of sunshine pours,
Mud clods and a boot-camp runt
having intercourse.

The residual magic
of depressing symposia;
everyone wants to absorb
the new eudemonia.

II

The biped of infinite size
has no room for the third leg,
where to have it grafted on,
instead,
decides to extemporize.

III

The forbidden parts of a dark,
lean, and longing night we see,
suspended bunches, wedges,
end in a comma, and then without
the comma, a whole new reality.

János Pilinszky

THE ANGEL OF BRIGHTNESS

Remembering a Christmas during a World War
(*A fenséges angyal*)

The vault of our sky turned dark.
It looked like the somber cloud
of Judgment Day had broken in,
and left us under darkness bowed.

Children's heart can be so heavy!
We wondered what managed to make
our fragile world around us tremble,
even houses and gardens quake.

And then in the giant silence,
softly and without a note at all,
without a sign it slowly began,
unnoticed, snow started to fall;

and, as carefully as the lustrous
snowflakes landed without a sound,
the light-bearing angel of brightness
slowly stepped down to the ground.

János Pilinszky

FABULA
(Fable)

Once upon a time there lived
a lone wolf in the woods.
Angels could not have been lonelier.

One day he wandered into a village
and fell in love with the first house he saw.

He even loved the walls,
the way the bricklayer had caressed the plaster,
but the window stopped him.

Inside the room people were sitting around.
Only god would've deemed them
as beautiful as
this pure-hearted beast did.

At night he stole into the house,
stopped in the middle of the room
and never made another move again.

With eyes open he stayed standing all night and
even in the morning when they beat him to death.

János Pilinszky

KNOCKING
(*Kopogtatnak*)

We were asleep. In my dream I was a tree,
then nothing, and then the kind of child
who knocks on an adult's door.
All this time you too were a tree. A child's skirt.
Not a door. Knocking. Rapping.
We were rapping together. I don't remember
if on the same door. One thing is sure:
the thrashing of a cherub must be like that.

László Nagy

FIRE

(*Tűz*)

Fire
that we can all admire
throbbing with the force of stars
you feed the engine till it dies,
drive it so that its black loneliness
will burn it that much less,
fire
that we can all admire,
idea flash, rooted in the universe,
go and flourish in bleeding birds,
burn it till it reveals our fate,
not in bones that incinerate,
a word awake is what we need,
fire
that we can all admire,
victoriously happy even on ice,
don't let aging make us weird
and our soul start to grow a beard,
in calculating, cold sobriety,
selling trade and treachery,
dress us up in fairyland-like red,
fly us past the stop sign dead,
in a dance of icebergs flung
you're the king of growing young,
fire!

László Nagy

WHO CAN FERRY LOVE ACROSS
(*Ki viszi át a Szerelmet*)

When life has at last done me in,
who'll admire a cricket violin?
Who breaths fire on wet twigs?
Who crucifies himself on rainbows?
Who embraces weeping rocky hips
into gently rolling meadows?
Who can fawn on hairs and veins
growing in hard walls in vain?
Using curses, who'll assemble
for wild creeds a sacred temple?
When life has at last done me in,
who will stop the vultures' din?
Held by his teeth without a loss,
who can ferry Love across?

Sándor Kányádi

BEHIND GOD'S BACK

(*Isten háta mögött*)

empty mangers empty stalls
christmas here no longer calls
no use waiting for
the wisemen at the door

the creator's got a lot to do
can't see to all those in the queue
far star is that sun
to shine on everyone

we know we must have faith in him
but the evenings are so dim
and the lack of loving care
leaves us feeling cold and bare

in foresight oh lord you don't lack
but take a look behind your back
we've been stuck here for a while
waiting for your blessing smile

1985

Sándor Kányádi

MISMATCHED AUTUMN LOVESONG
(*Felemás őszi ének*)

every night you must rebuild
everything that's easy prey
inside you to the wreckage wreaked
by the battles of the day

don't let the fire go out no matter
how many times it's trampled down
because without you rekindling them
the remaining embers too will drown

what I'm saying is old news
it's all been televised and aired
the dry and stingy summer has left us
facing winter unprepared

I only try to save myself
in you and also you in me
as long as heaven wants us to play
this mortal human comedy

1992

Gizella Hervay

NAKED BEFORE INTERROGATION LIGHTS

(*Meztelenül a vallatófényben*)

we're denied the shelter of darkness and silent grief
naked before interrogation lights
just how many eyes do we have? how many ears?
who can recognize one's lover?
when in trouble who'll take a chance and call mother?
christs that can't be resurrected
denuded of halo
shoved into a battlefield trench
orphan targets of the future
the word sliced off the mouth
with remote-controlled breathing
in pain that can't be shared
hung out for one last howl
with grillwork around the lungs
we're denied the shelter of darkness and silent grief

Gizella Hervay

DEFENSELESS

(*Védtelenül*)

You know it's only my lot that's beastly,
and yet you leave me in disdain.
I watch the thickening mist in your eyes.
You're cruel, it's only my lot that's inhumane.
I'm cruel, how can I ask you
to share my screwed-up life.

Can one remain human
locked into an inhumane lot?
Shall I give up your smile?
Shall I slap your face with love?

Desire is as defenseless
as a naked thought.

We long for purity too fiercely
that it ends up besmirching us.

Goodness is as hard to see
as death seeping into a flower.

It hurts my hands to stroke a tree bark.
Does it hurt the tree to be stroked?
Does it hurt you to be stroked?

Desire is as defenseless
as a naked thought.

And purity is as hard to see
as death seeping into a flower.

Gizella Hervay

THE GUARDIAN

(*Vigyázó*)

There are those who can hear a blade of grass emerge;
I can hear a thought suddenly rear its head.

There are those who go without sleep so as to reach the sea of dawn;
and I can never be indifferent,
after all,
any unknown thought may turn against us;
any unknown thought may explode,
in a matter if seconds only the shadows of our bodies are left
on granite slabs.

There are those who water flowers at dusk;
I sit out on the stoops of eyes.

SPRING

(*Tavasz*)

The spring too is one of her chores,
that's why she walks around so quietly,
with silent fingers;
in her hands mornings are born ahead of time,
even before the clatter of milk-bottle dawns.
Garish truck convoys follow in her wake,
but she keeps walking with a smile.
She projects the shadows of spaceships and
cement-glass poems on the century's forehead.
Why would she take home a bunch of violets?
She knows: she's tempted by ultraviolet life,
so she keeps working with clenched fists.
The sky is a halo erected over her head.

Gizella Hervay

RESUME
(Űrlap)

I grew up, didn't I. That means we should re-do
the resume. There was too much vagrancy
connected with being an orphan, and too
few were the homes available per person.
This we must re-write. Yes, I'm at home here.
I create my own landscape. Out of words,
of course. Out of good, sturdy words.
They can be size eleven, too, but they must be
boots. Without boots you can't march off
to war. But of course, that's
over now. And an overcoat
is also important in this area. It's safe
and secure like childhood. Which I didn't have.
It can be long, too. We can always tuck
it in. One can grow out of them by the end
of their useful lives. Out of poems,
of course. The rest we can cross out. Please
cross it out. Just leave the bare facts. Please take
this down: I was born like others. I accept the
responsibility. According to
Central-European calendar.
Let me have a copy, please.

APPENDIX

BLACK-BELTED SHADOW

(*Paraphrase on Endre Ady's poem "The Black-Lacquered Concert Grand"*)

A frivolously murdered night
whose resurrection every fable felt:
the black-leather garter belt.
Its master blindly twirls his stick
for history's hoariest magic trick:
the black-leather garter belt.

The dearest gasp of an unlived life
spread-eagled in an open welt;
all that and more, the garter belt.
Instead of blood try purging the pain
inside your heart with pure champagne;
the black-leather garter-belt.

A hymn-hemmed sin, baptismal shroud,
the halo that will make you melt,
the black-leather garter belt;
the mask of the lewd rigmarole
that will hang you by the soul,
the black-leather garter belt.

A POET'S COMMENTS ON PILLARS OF MAGYAR POETRY

Paul Sohar's fascination with Hungarian literature and deep love of Magyar history are brought to the fore in this rewarding collection that does not stop with poetry. While the language has survived over the centuries, the boundaries of the nation have expanded and contracted countless times, as is the natural course of power and influence of nations.

The author's unique approach to this fact is reflected in the selections of works he has translated over decades, chosen specifically here to represent the affects of the stressors of war on the people and the poets of their respective generations. A preface that explains the more profound social, cultural and religious influences from within and without the Magyar tribes lays stones in the road to understanding why he chose the poets and poems included in the anthology, as well as to understanding the poems themselves.

Paul's abiding preoccupation to present their words stylistically, and with attention to emotional intent, is a task native speakers are best prepared to bring about. I have read other translations of some of the same poems in this collection and find while others are appealing in their results, Paul's work seems to hold more to the original... To wit:

Sohar's translation of Razglednicák, said to be the final poem by Miklós Radnót found in his jacket pocket on his body found in a mass grave during the Holocaust: Postcard 4 of 4...

> I hit the ground beside his corpse; it flipped,
> already as stiff as a string about to break.
> Shot in the back of the head. "You'll be next",
> I told myself. "Just lie still, without a quake.
> It's death that blooms from patience here."
> *"Der spingt noch auf,"* someone barked above.
> A crust of blood and mud dried up on my ear.

And, as loosely translated by Michael R. Burch:

I toppled beside him—his body already taut,
tight as a string just before it snaps,
shot in the back of the head.
"This is how you'll end too; just lie quietly here,"
I whispered to myself, patience blossoming from dread.
"Der springt noch auf," the voice above me jeered;
I could only dimly hear
through the congealing blood slowly sealing my ear.

Especially evident to me was the contemporary sense I was left with after reading the poems of 20th Century poet Gizella Hervay, incidentally the only woman whose works are included in the book.

THE GUARDIAN (*Vigyázó*)

There are those who can hear a blade of grass emerge;
I can hear a thought suddenly rear its head.

There are those who go without sleep so as to reach the sea of dawn;
and I can never be indifferent,
after all,
any unknown thought may turn against us;
any unknown thought may explode,
in a matter if seconds only the shadows of our bodies are left
on granite slabs.

There are those who water flowers at dusk;
I sit out on the stoops of eyes.

Compare the free verse in the translation of Hervay's poem with the classical strains in Sándor Petőfi's "My Winter...":

MY WINTER IN DEBRECZEN (*Egy telem Debreczenben*)

Hey, you, town of Debreczen,
how often you taunt my mind
with the suffering you gave to me!...
And yet you remain
a beloved and kind
old guest in my memory.

A papist I am surely not,
yet I fasted there a lot.
Good thing the gods made mortal teeth
out of bone by wise design. No doubt,
had my teeth been made of steel,
they would've surely rusted out.

This latest book is another in the long line of Sohar's translations that bring his birth nation's history, heart, and soul to the English reader. As the son of an Hungarian immigrant who like Paul arrived in the States as an émigré, my father escaping the Holocaust and Paul the 1956 Revolution, I did not learn Magyar as a child. Sohar's work has provided a link to their and my same shared past. Do not take that to mean one needs to be Hungarian to appreciate what can be found in these works, for it's the love and loss that lifts or lowers the humanity we find imbued in true poetry. And that is what the Pillars are about.

Michael Foldes, Editor of *Ragazine*, Endwell, NY

ACKNOWLEDGEMENTS

At least in part, the purpose of this anthology is to preserve translations that have not made their way into print, but a few already published poems just demanded inclusion. Grateful acknowledgement is expressed here to the editors of those hospitable publications that have brought them to the world.

Big Hammer: All poems by Kassák
Bitter Oleander: The Crimson Cart at Sea (Ady)
Consequences: Cadaver on the Wheatfield, The New Harvest Song (Ady)
Dancing Embers: Behind God's Back (Kányádi)
Down Fell the Statue of Goliath (Anthology): Tyranny in One Sentence (Illyés)
Exit 13: Burial at Sea, The Wasteland of Hungary (Ady)
Frisson: I've Killed a Butterfly (Ady)
Homing Poems (Translator's poems, Iniquity Press: Poems by Ady, József, Radnóti, Faludy)
Hungarian Poetry Review: The Song of a Grieving Hungarian (József),
The Church and the School (Reményik)
Hungarian Poets Cry out to the Poets of Europe (Kosztolányi)
In Contemporary Tense: Mismatched Autumn Love Song (Kányádi)
International Poetry Review: Love Sonnet (Faludy)
Language and Culture: Naked before Interrogation Lights (Hervay)
Loch Raven Review: Resume (Hervay)
Maelstrom: Ceremony (Hervay)
National Translation Month: To Hope, etc. (Csokonai),
Longing to Belong, etc. (Ady),
There's No Money and We Must Eat, etc. (Szabó)
Pedestal: Angel from Heaven (Márai)
Pilvax: Duel with the Hog-Headed Mister Big, etc. (Ady)
Poetry Depth Quarterly: Leda's Heart (Ady)
Rhino: On New Waters I Sail (Ady)
Silver Pirouettes (a book of poems by Faludy, Ragged Sky Press): Farewell to Recsk
Translation: The Cousin of Death (Ady)
Visions International: Spring (Hervay)
Writers Journal: The Black-Lacquered Concert Grand (Ady)
Zymbol: Remembering a Summer Night (Ady)

ABOUT THE TRANSLATOR

Paul Sohar (born 1936, in Hungary) found his way as a 1956 refugee to the United States where he continued his studies in philosophy and chemistry. The latter subject secured for him a day job in a research lab, but at night he immersed himself in literature. After early retirement on disability, his sporadic publications grew to an avalanche of poetry, prose, and translations. His own poetry has appeared in three books, one of them a prize winner *Wayward Orchard* (Wordrunner Press, 2011), and the latest being *In Sun's Shadow* (Ragged Sky Press, 2020). His nineteen volumes of translations have earned him four prizes, most recently the ***Balassi Literary Translation Grand Prize*** (2021, Budapest, Hungary). His writings and translations have appeared in hundreds of periodicals such as *Agni, Kenyon Review, Rhino, Writers Journal,* and others.

www.ingramcontent.com/pod-product-compliance
Lightning Source LLC
LaVergne TN
LVHW090948080826
845145LV00003B/931
9781950063864